WHAT HAPPENS NEXT

ALSO BY MAX LUCADO

Inspirational

3:16
A Gentle Thunder
A Love Worth Giving
And the Angels Were Silent
Anxious for Nothing
Because of Bethlehem
Before Amen
Come Thirsty
Cure for the Common Life
Facing Your Giants
Fearless
Glory Days
God Came Near
God Never Gives Up on You
Grace
Great Day Every Day
He Chose the Nails
He Still Moves Stones
Help Is Here
How Happiness Happens
In the Eye of the Storm
In the Grip of Grace
It's Not About Me
Just Like Jesus
Max on Life
More to Your Story
Next Door Savior
No Wonder They Call Him the Savior
On the Anvil
Outlive Your Life
Six Hours One Friday
The Applause of Heaven
The Great House of God
Traveling Light
Unshakable Hope
When Christ Comes
When God Whispers Your Name
You Are Never Alone
You'll Get Through This
You Were Made for This Moment

Compilations

Begin Again
In the Footsteps of the Savior
Jesus
Start with Prayer
They Walked with God

Fiction

Christmas Stories
Miracle at the Higher Grounds Café
The Christmas Candle

Bibles (General Editor)

The Lucado Encouraging Word Bible
Children's Daily Devotional Bible
Grace for the Moment Daily Bible
The Lucado Life Lessons Study Bible

Children's Books

A Max Lucado Children's Treasury
Bedtime Prayers for Little Ones
God Always Keeps His Promises
God Forgives Me, and I Forgive You
Grace for the Moment: 365 Devotions for Kids
Hermie, a Common Caterpillar
I'm Not a Scaredy Cat
Itsy Bitsy Christmas
Just in Case You Ever Wonder
Just in Case You Ever Feel Alone
Lucado Treasury of Bedtime Prayers
One Hand, Two Hands
Thank You, God, for Blessing Me
Thank You, God, for Loving Me
The Crippled Lamb
The Oak Inside the Acorn
You Are Special
Where'd My Giggle Go?

Young Adult Books

3:16
It's Not About Me
Make Every Day Count
Wild Grace
You Were Made to Make a Difference
Anxious for Nothing (Young Readers Edition)
One God, One Plan, One Life
Unshakable Hope Promise Book
You Can Count on God

Gift Books

Calm Moments for Anxious Days
Fear Not Promise Book
God Is with You Every Day
God Thinks You're Wonderful
God Will Help You
Grace for the Moment
Grace for the Moment Family Devotional
Grace for the Moment for Moms
Grace Happens Here
Happy Today
Let the Journey Begin
Live Loved
Praying the Promises
Safe in the Shepherd's Arms
Trade Your Cares for Calm
You Can Count on God

WHAT HAPPENS NEXT

A TRAVELER'S GUIDE THROUGH THE END OF THIS AGE

MAX LUCADO

THOMAS NELSON
Since 1798

What Happens Next

Published in Nashville, Tennessee, by Thomas Nelson. Thomas Nelson is a registered trademark of HarperCollins Christian Publishing, Inc.

Thomas Nelson titles may be purchased in bulk for educational, business, fundraising, or sales promotional use. For information please e-mail SpecialMarkets@ThomasNelson.com.

ISBN 978-1-4002-6002-7 (audiobook)
ISBN 978-1-4002-6001-0 (eBook)
ISBN 978-1-4002-5117-9 (IE)
ISBN 978-1-4002-6000-3 (HC)

Library of Congress Cataloging-in-Publication Data

Names: Lucado, Max, author.
Title: What happens next : a traveler's guide through the end of this age / Max Lucado.
Description: Nashville, Tennessee : Thomas Nelson, [2024] | Summary: "Are we living in the end times? If so, what does that mean for me? Max Lucado's optimistic, accessible, and non-sensational guide to what the Bible says about heaven's timeline will empower readers to face the future with faith"-- Provided by publisher.
Identifiers: LCCN 2024011237 (print) | LCCN 2024011238 (ebook) | ISBN 9781400260003 (hardcover) | ISBN 9781400260010 (epub) | ISBN 9781400260027 (audiobook)
Subjects: LCSH: End of the world. | Eschatology.
Classification: LCC BT877 .L83 2024 (print) | LCC BT877 (ebook) | DDC 236/.9--dc23/eng/20240323
LC record available at https://lccn.loc.gov/2024011237
LC ebook record available at https://lccn.loc.gov/2024011238

Printed in the United States of America

24 25 26 27 28 LBC 10 9 8 7 6

Denalyn and I would like to dedicate this volume to our wonderful friends at HarperCollins Christian Publishing. For decades we have been the beneficiaries of their kindness, professionalism, and commitment to quality. We are honored to know them and celebrate their great work.

Contents

Acknowledgments

AN EXTRAORDINARY COLLECTION of friends and colleagues contributed to this book. They offered advice, answered questions, corrected my misdirections, and gave ample words of encouragement. Let me introduce them to you.

My editorial assistant, Karen Hill—we've worked together for over three decades. She's heard more Lucado lessons and read more Lucado chapters than any person on the planet. She is a saint and I'm forever grateful.

My editor, Sam O'Neal—unflappable, calming, and capable. If this book brings clarity, it is largely due to Sam's innate ability to help a writer stay on task and avoid rabbit trails. Thank you, Sam.

Steve and Cheryl Green manage my publishing, broadcasting, online ministry . . . they manage me! And they manage everything with joy!

A cohort of colleagues from the church where I serve met with me each week for several months. They read each chapter in advance. Together we prayed, pored over passages, and pursued biblical truth. A loud thank-you to Travis Eades, Jeremy Jennings, Pat Hile, Matt Moore, and Rick Nicosia.

Three scholars were kind enough to review this manuscript and offer their thoughts: Mark Hitchcock, Matt Queen, and David Drury. These friends were generous with their time, honest with their input. When we disagreed, they were gracious; when we agreed, they were affirming. I deeply appreciate each of you.

O. S. Hawkins, Jimmy Evans, and David Jeremiah were always a call or text away. Each one a serious student of the Bible. Each one a cheerleader and friend.

Special gratitude to my longtime copy editor Carol Bartley, with highest admiration.

Great appreciation to Rhonda Lowry for checking and double checking sources, and to Phil Newman, Kelsey Mitchener, and Kristin Spann for proofreading the manuscript. Thank you for cleaning up after me. Elena de Medina translated this book into Spanish, and, in doing so, made valuable suggestions. Gracias!

Jana Muntsinger and Pamela McClure—peerless publicists. I'm grateful.

The team at HarperCollins Christian Publishing is the gold standard. I'm indebted to Mark Schoenwald, Don Jacobson, Andrew Stoddard, Mark Glesne, Bria Woods, Janene MacIvor, Laura Minchew, Doug Lockhart, Mark Weising, and Dave Schroeder.

A special thanks to creative artists Emily Ghattas and Curt Diepenhorst for designing this book, and to Layne Pittman and David Feagan for producing the audiobook.

Greg, Susan, and Daniel Ligon have the extraordinary capacity to spin innumerable plates and corral a herd of stallions. I'm in awe of you.

Here is a standing ovation for Caroline Green, overseer of the *Encouraging Word Podcast* and all-around brilliant associate.

Margaret Mechinus and Janie Padilla keep their wings hidden away, but don't be fooled. They are angels on loan from heaven.

Years ago, I began inviting David Treat, an elder from our church, to the final editing session. He gives up two or three days each year to sit in the corner of the room and pray while we work. A picture of a servant.

Brett, Jenna, Rosie, Max, Rob, Andrea, Rio, Jeff, Sara, and June. Our family keeps growing and so does my love.

Denalyn, my bride. You're everything I ever want to do and be. I love you.

And you, dear reader. Thank you. May God bless you on this exploration of what happens next. The topic is so exciting and invigorating. I offer a prayer for you.

One final word. I have a reserved seat at the PWPOET Café in heaven—**P**astors **W**ho **P**reached **O**n **E**nd **T**imes. We will celebrate what we understood correctly, chuckle at what we missed entirely. Mostly, we will honor the one Teacher who stands above us all, Jesus Christ.

HEAVEN'S TIME LINE

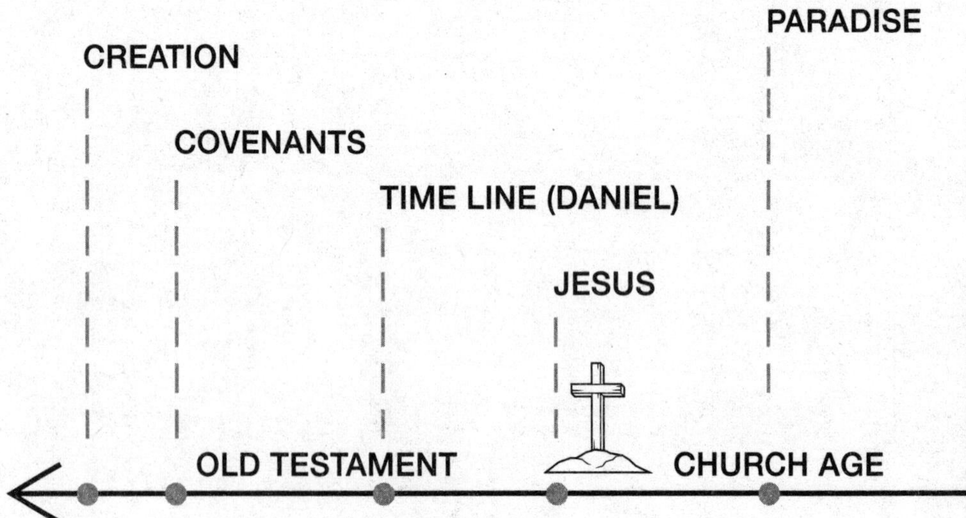

NOT TO SCALE

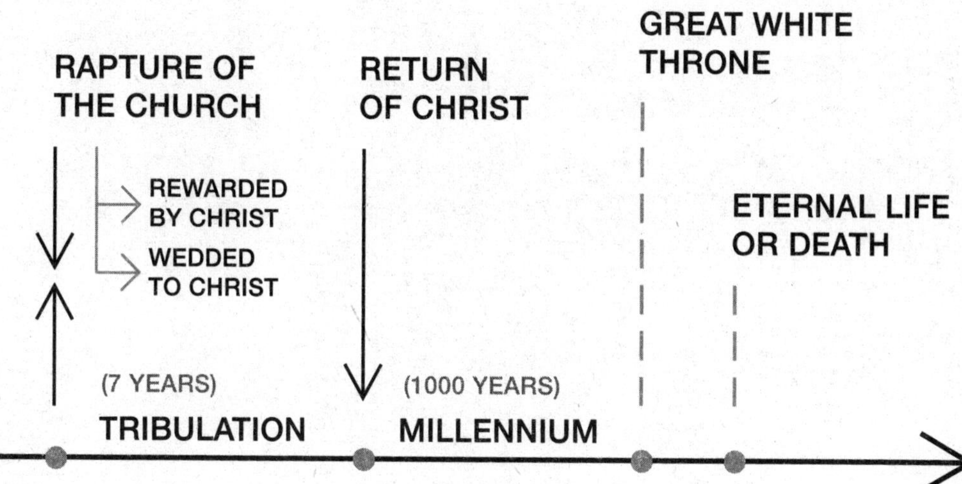
GREAT WHITE THRONE
RAPTURE OF THE CHURCH
RETURN OF CHRIST
REWARDED BY CHRIST
WEDDED TO CHRIST
ETERNAL LIFE OR DEATH
(7 YEARS)
TRIBULATION
(1000 YEARS)
MILLENNIUM

CHAPTER 1

Good to Go

YOU'VE SELECTED YOUR CLOTHING. You've checked the weather and chosen your jacket. Toiletries are packed. Suitcase is fastened. Hotel is confirmed. Your boarding pass is downloaded. Your ride to the airport is waiting. Before you walk out the door, you pause to inventory your list.

Water bottle? Got it.

Spending money? Got it.

Smartphone? Book to read? Journal and pen? Check. Check. Check.

You are good to go.

There may be surprises along the way. Unexpected eventualities. Interruptions here. Changes there. Delays, disruptions, detours. You can't know everything that will happen. But you've done all you can do to prepare. You've made your plans, reviewed the itinerary, and anticipated the journey. You are equipped. You are ready.

You're good to go.

Wouldn't it be foolish not to be?

I've done my share of travel through the decades. I've trudged through dozens of airports. Slept in too many hotels to count. I've worn out the wheels of a roller bag. In the process, I've spoken to hundreds of travelers. I consider myself a bit of an expert in airport repartee. It typically consists of one question.

"Where are you headed?"

There you have it. You are hereby equipped for travel chitchat. That question is for a traveler what a spoon is for a chef. I use it often.

I've heard hundreds of answers. "Toledo." "Rio." "Tokyo." "Kokomo." But I've never, ever heard this reply: "I don't know."

Not once has someone said, "I have no clue."

Travelers know their destination, right? Travel 101 instructs, "Know where you go."

Wouldn't Life 101 say the same?

We are all headed somewhere. Each day brings us closer to a final breath, a final heartbeat, a final sigh. No one is getting younger. Death comes to the young, the old, the rich, the poor, the decent, the decadent, the king, and the commoner. Shouldn't our destination be an obsession?

The Bible certainly suggests as much. It makes almost five hundred references to heaven.[1] The New Testament mentions the return of Jesus more than three hundred times—one out of every thirty verses! Twenty-three of the twenty-seven books in the New Testament describe Jesus' second coming, and on some fifty occasions we are told to be ready.[2]

If quantity equates to priority, then life after this life is a crucial issue to God.

Canvass the Scripture's teaching about the future, and two themes repeatedly surface.

It's All About Hope

On the eve of his crucifixion, Jesus told his followers what was going to happen the following day. He would be abandoned by his friends and killed by his enemies. Denial, betrayal, broken promises, and death.

What news could be worse for them? Their rabbi, dead. The apostles, alone. Their dreams, ended. Questions rose in their minds like waves on a stormy sea.

"How can this be?"

"What does he mean?"

"Where shall we go?"

Yet before they could voice their fears, Jesus calmed them.

"Do not let your hearts be troubled. You believe in God; believe also in me. My Father's house has many rooms; if that were not so, would I have told you that I am going there to prepare a place for you? And if I go and prepare a place for you, I will come back and take you to be with me that you also may be where I am" (John 14:1–3).

Note what Jesus did. He lifted their eyes; he shifted their thoughts. He spoke of his Father's house, a prepared place, and his promised return. In essence he said, "Think less about your present fears. Think much about your eternal home." What would Jesus say to this troubled generation of ours?

Hope is an endangered species. We are more troubled than we've been in nearly fifty years. Only 14 percent of respondents check the "very happy" box on the survey questionnaire. We are less optimistic about the future than we've been in three decades. "Nearly one in four people—which translates to a billion people—feels very or fairly lonely."[3] Happiness is down. Loneliness is up. And optimism has taken a right hook to the chin.

Most alarming is the absence of peace among our youth. Research from the National Institute of Mental Health (NIMH) is showing an epidemic of mental health problems among eighteen- to twenty-four-year-olds in the United States.

- One out of four shows symptoms of anxiety disorder.[4]
- One in eight young adults (13 percent) has experienced serious suicidal thoughts.[5]
- One in seven young adults deals with a substance-use disorder, including drugs or alcohol.[6]
- Overall, half of college-aged individuals indicate they regularly experience anxiety, depression, fear, or suicidal thoughts.[7]
- Today's young adults—tomorrow's generation of leaders—are struggling to find meaning and purpose in their lives.[8]
- The suicide rate is the highest it has been since World War II.[9]

You can relate. Your heart has been broken. Your dreams have been shattered. Your body has battled disease and aging. And maybe you've wondered, really wondered, if this life is worth living.

God's therapy for our trepidation reads like this:

> For our present troubles are small and won't last very long. Yet they produce for us a glory that vastly outweighs them and will last forever! So we don't look at the troubles we can see now; rather, we fix our gaze on things that cannot be seen. For the things we see now will soon be gone, but the things we cannot see will last forever. (2 Cor. 4:17–18 NLT)

Face the problems of this life by focusing on the promises of the next.

Face the problems of this life by focusing on the promises of the next. The future is not as frightening if you know the future. And you can know the future when you know who controls it.

It's All About Him

On the day Jesus ascended into heaven, two angels appeared and asked the watching followers this question: "Men of Galilee, why do you stand looking into the sky? This Jesus, who has been taken up from you into heaven, will come in just the same way as you have watched Him go into heaven" (Acts 1:11 NASB).

Jesus will come! Not "may come," "might come," or "possibly could come." Jesus will come! His promised return is not a nebulous, vapid, cross-your-fingers aspiration. It is a concrete, guaranteed appearance of our Savior.

Jesus validated his return by vacating his tomb. This was the conviction of the apostle Paul:

> If there's no resurrection for Christ, everything we've told you is smoke and mirrors, and everything you've staked your life on is smoke and mirrors. . . . If all we get out of Christ is a little inspiration for a few short years, we're a pretty sorry lot. But the truth is that Christ *has* been

> raised up, the first in a long legacy of those who are going to leave the cemeteries. (1 Cor. 15:14, 19–20 MSG)

Is the tomb of Jesus empty? Did he defang death? Did Christ discard his shrouds like a bad habit and march out of the tomb?

The women who came to the tomb would say, "Yes! We saw him!" (John 20:11–17; Matt. 28:9–10).

His disciples who gathered in the Upper Room would say, "Yes! We saw him!" (John 20:19–29).

Five hundred followers would say, "Yes! We saw him!" (1 Cor. 15:6).

"Line them up!" invites the New Testament. "Ask the followers if Jesus rose from the dead."

The resounding answer is "Yes." His tomb floor has the prints of pierced feet. Those feet were nailed to a cross on Friday and lifeless in the grave on Saturday. But on Sunday the hope of Easter called them to stand, step, and walk out of the grave.

When Jesus vacated the tomb, he populated the heart of humanity with hope. Since his grave is empty, our confidence in his return is not.

Peter spent most of his remaining years living in Jerusalem. How many times did he take the brief walk to the Mount of Olives and reflect on the words of the angel? "He will come back." Did he search the clouds? Contemplate the heavens? Reflect on the angel's promise? "Jesus . . . will come in just the same way as you have watched Him go."

Three decades later he urged his readers to do so. "Set your hope completely on the grace to be brought to you at the revelation of Jesus Christ" (1 Peter 1:13 NASB).

The Christian lives life on tiptoe, ever searching the skies. We awaken with the thought *Perhaps today!* Our hope is centered on the bodily return of Christ. We are looking to a new age in which Jesus will be crowned as the rightful King and we will serve as his grateful servants. All of history is headed to the great day that will inaugurate an endless era of justice, joy, and glory.

In one of his earliest sermons, Peter declared: "The Lord will . . . send Jesus, the One he chose to be the Christ. But Jesus must stay in heaven until the time comes when all things will be made right again" (Acts 3:19–21 NCV).

Things will be made right again. Does that assurance not speak to the heavy heart? Weary of racism? *Things will be made right.* Weary of child abuse? *Things will be made right.* Weary of terrorists wreaking terror? Rulers pillaging the poor? Scandal infecting the church? *Things . . . will . . . be . . . made . . . right.*

This is our hope. *He* is our hope. "Christ Jesus . . . is our hope" (1 Tim. 1:1 NASB). Follow the counsel of Paul: "Set your mind on things above, not on things on the earth" (Col. 3:2 NKJV). I disagree with the person who says, "We can be so heavenly minded that we are no earthly good." Hogwash. "If you read history," C. S. Lewis wrote, "you will find that the Christians who did most for the present world were just those who thought most of the next." He added: "The Apostles themselves, who set on foot the conversion of the Roman Empire, the great men who built up the Middle Ages, the English Evangelicals who abolished the Slave Trade, all left their mark on Earth, precisely because their minds were occupied with Heaven."[10]

I told a friend that I was writing a book about the end times. He responded with cynicism. "Why think about the future? I'm a *carpe diem* sort of dude. I'd rather focus on the here and now." Valid point. We have bills to pay, kids to raise, deadlines to meet. Why occupy our thoughts with the "not yet" when we need strength to face the "right now"?

Simple. Understanding the future empowers us to face the present. That was Paul's opinion: "I focus on this one thing: Forgetting the past and looking forward to what lies ahead, I press on to reach the end of the race and receive the heavenly prize for which God, through Christ Jesus, is calling us" (Phil. 3:13–14 NLT).

Look at those phrases: "looking forward to what lies ahead," "end of the race," "heavenly prize." The best of life is yet to be. Got challenges in this life? Then ponder the next. Be a future-facing follower of Christ.

Besides, don't we yearn to know about the future? I do.

I'm genuinely curious about what happens next. Maybe because I'm getting older. My next birthday cake will require room for seventy candles. I'll need a fire extinguisher to blow them out. My hair is grayer, and my bald spot is larger. My hourglass has much more sand on the bottom than on the top. Consequently, eschatology (the study of end times) has become a fascination for me. Odd, I know. Some people take up gardening or painting as they get older; I've taken up questions about the rapture, the Antichrist, and Armageddon. I really, really want to know what's around the corner.

I'm curious about the future.

I'm also concerned about the present. Who wouldn't be? As I write these words, the United States lives under the threat of conflict with Iran or China or Russia or all three. Israel is at war with Hamas, and Hezbollah is rattling sabers against Israel. We could add a cluster of other concerns: shifting weather patterns, pandemics, and famine. Our fragile condition has prompted a group to monitor the possibility of global catastrophe. Their latest estimate? We are "ninety seconds to midnight."[11]

Quite a mess, right? It's no wonder four in ten Americans believe we are living in end times.[12] We are looking at a very severe future. Yet, Jesus told us to anticipate choppy waters.

According to him, the final days will be marked by escalating events of . . .

- deception
- signs in the heavens
- economic turmoil
- seismic activity
- persecution of Christians
- political conflict
- famines
- pestilence
- commotions
- ethnic conflicts
- false prophets
- waning faith
- fearful sights
- wars and rumors of wars
- diseases (Matt. 24:4–14; Mark 13:5–13; Luke 21:11)

Sounds like the daily news. Jesus said, "All these events are the beginning of the labor pains" (Matt. 24:8 CSB).

I have it on good authority that labor pains increase in frequency and intensity as the delivery draws near. Jesus was speaking of a day in which the same will happen in the world. There will be a generation in which danger and depravity escalate at an increasing rate.

Are we living in that era? In other words . . .

Is This the Fourth Quarter?

I believe it is. Something happened on Friday, May 14, 1948, that differentiates this era from any other in human history.

On that day two men sat in a quiet corner of the F Street Club in Washington, DC, and worked out the wording of a statement soon to be released by the White House. One of the men was Harry Truman. He had become president of the United States when Franklin Roosevelt died early in his fourth term. The next few years led Truman into one of the most tumultuous chapters of American history. Under his leadership World War II came to an end, the United Nations was formed, the US military was desegregated, and the Marshall Plan was born. He was president during the surrenders of Germany and Japan. He witnessed the fall of the Iron Curtain over Eastern Europe and the Bamboo Curtain over China and parts of East Asia.

Yet, of all Truman's decisions, none more hearkened into the past or bore more implications for the eternal future than the one he and his special counsel Clark Clifford had met to discuss. At issue was the confirmation of a Jewish state. Though much of his administration, including his secretary of state, opposed such a step, Truman was resolved. Himself a Christian, he had sought the counsel of prominent pastor J. Frank Norris of Fort Worth, Texas.[13]

Norris reminded the president of God's promise to Isaac: "Live here as a foreigner in this land, and I will be with you and bless you. I hereby confirm that I will give all these lands to you and your descendants, just as I solemnly promised Abraham, your father" (Gen. 26:3 NLT).

Truman sent Pastor Norris a thank-you note. Shortly thereafter he made his decision.

Having hammered out the best wording for the statement, Clifford put through a hurried call to Elihu Epstein, an official at the Jewish agency in Washington, to tell him that recognition would occur later that day. "The New Jewish state—the first Jewish state in nearly 2,000 years—was declared on schedule at midnight in Jerusalem, 6:00 p.m. in Washington. Eleven minutes later at the White House, Charlie Ross announced *de facto* recognition by the United States."[14]

The president signed a two-paragraph proclamation that read: "This government has been informed that a Jewish state has been proclaimed in Palestine, and recognition has been requested by the provisional government thereof. The United States recognizes the provisional government as the de facto authority of the new state of Israel."

The name "state of Israel" was handwritten because the name of the nation was not chosen until the last minute.

What other nation has been promised land by God, been removed from the land, and then returned to it? The answer: none. Yet, this reinstatement was promised in Scripture.

From Ezekiel, 650 years before Christ: "For I will take you from the nations and gather you from all the lands, and bring you into your own land" (Ezek. 36:24 NLV).

From Isaiah, 740 years before Christ: "He will raise a banner for the nations and gather the exiles of Israel; he will assemble the scattered people of Judah from the four quarters of the earth" (Isa. 11:12).[15]

May 14, 1948, saw a page turn in the calendar of prophetic history. Circumstances changed when the Jews were given their land. As we will discuss in the following pages, almost all the key events of the end times hinge upon the existence of Israel as a nation.

- The book of Daniel prophesies a covenant between the Antichrist and Israel (Dan. 9:27). This can only happen if the nation of Israel exists.
- Scripture prophesies a rebuilding of the temple (Isa. 2:1–4; 2 Thess. 2:4). Again, Israel must exist for this to happen.
- Daniel and Jesus forecast an act of utter sacrilege in the temple (Dan. 12:11; Mark 13:14). No Israel, no temple.
- The war of Armageddon only makes sense if Israel is occupying the land where that particular valley (called Megiddo) is found.

Prior to 1948 a Jewish repopulation of Israel as a state was unthinkable. Jews were dispersed to more than seventy countries for more than twenty centuries. Yet since 1948 we have seen them return. For the first time since AD 135, there are more Jews living in Israel than in any other place on earth.

This resettlement is often referred to as a "super sign." The Bible repeatedly presents the regathering of Jewish people as a watershed event that must occur before other end-times events take place (Jer. 30:1–5; Ezek. 34:11–24; Ezek. 37; Zech. 10:6–10). It is akin to the flag wave at a NASCAR race signaling the final lap. Other signs take on heightened importance now that the super sign has occurred. We've always had wars, disasters, and deceptions. But now that the milestone moment has happened and Israel is restored, the other signs progressively signal the impending end.

If history is a year, the leaves are autumn gold.

If history is a day, the sun has begun to set.

If history is an hour, the hands of the clock are nearing full circle.

We have entered the last days. So, let us be looking. Let us be declaring: the end is near.

This was my job on the high school football team. I was one of the players who declared the onset of the fourth quarter. There were five of us, maybe six. We were the misfits on the varsity squad. Not bad enough to be cut. By no means good enough to play. In the football dog pound, we were the mongrels.

But we had our moment. And that moment came at the opening of the fourth quarter of each game.

Our assignment, on the coach's signal, was to run up and down the sideline with four fingers in the air shouting, "Fourth quarter! Fourth quarter!"

Teams tend to grow weary as the game wears on. The minutes take their toll. Players need a wake-up call. *This is the last push before the end. Dig deep! Be alert!*

Someone needed to yell, "Fourth quarter!" So, we did.

Doesn't the same need to be declared today?

Christ could come at any moment. I believe that with all my heart—not just because of what I read in the Scriptures, but also because of what I read in the news.

To be clear, "No one knows about that day or hour, not even the angels

We have entered the last days. So, let us be looking. Let us be declaring: the end is near.

in heaven, nor the Son, but only the Father" (Matt. 24:36 BSB). The exact time remains hidden. While we cannot know the day or hour, we can know the signs. Wouldn't you agree that the signs of our day warrant our vigilance?

We have a choice. We can view the future through the eyes of fear or faith. The eyes of fear see little reason for hope and ample reason for anxiety. The eyes of faith see history inching closer and closer to a new era, a heavenly destiny. God tells us what to expect not to scare us, but to prepare us. He is the pilot on the intercom telling the passengers about impending turbulence. A good pilot keeps his travelers informed. Our good Father does the same.

Between now and the end of this age we can expect some severe instability. But we will arrive safely.

Maybe you are a bit leery about this discussion. End-times studies have left you confused, perhaps cynical. I understand. Prophecy is to the Bible what the Serengeti is to Africa—vast, expansive, and intimidating. It's a world of numbers and symbols, bears and tigers. Most students prefer the domesticated, well-traveled streets of Scripture: the teachings of Jesus, the doctrines of Paul, the biographies of the Patriarchs. Prophecy intimidates many Bible students.

God tells us what to expect not to scare us, but to prepare us.

It infatuates others. If Bible prophecy is the Serengeti, some Christians are big-game hunters. They never leave the bush. They find prophecy on every page, symbolism in every story, and clues in every verse. They can be a great source of help, but they can also be stubbornly opinionated. Prophetic experts tend to be very confident; they walk with a game-hunter swagger. They always seem to know (and enjoy knowing) what others don't.

Somewhere in between these two positions is a healthy posture. Believers who avoid utter ignorance on one hand and total arrogance on the other. Who seek what God intends: a deep-seated confidence that our tomorrow is in our Lord's hands. The purpose of prophecy is to empower the saint with a sense of God's sovereignty. As Paul wrote: "But one who prophesies strengthens others, encourages them, and comforts them" (1 Cor. 14:3 NLT). Prophecy prepares us to face the future with faith.

Five hundred years ago sailors feared the horizon. Sail too far and risk falling off the edge, they reasoned. The common wisdom of the ancients warned against the unseen. So did the monument at the Strait of Gibraltar, where Spaniards held dominion over both sides of the strait. At its narrowest margin, where Africa can see Europe, they erected the Pillar of Hercules, a huge marker that bore in its stone the three-word Latin slogan *Ne plus ultra.* No More Beyond.

But then came Columbus and the voyage of 1492. The discovery of the new world swung open the western doors of Spain. They took the Latin phrase "No More Beyond," removed the first word, and impressed this slogan onto their coins: "More Beyond."[16]

Remove the "no" from your future. Open your heart and open your life to the great assurances. You were made to explore what happens next. It's all about hope. It's all about him.

Let's make sure we are good to go.

PART 1

Four Big Ideas

THE "FLIGHT TO NOWHERE" sold out in ten minutes. Qantas Airways called it the fastest-selling ticket in the airline's history. Cheap seats were priced at $575, and first-class seats sold for $2,675. What did passengers get for their money? Seven hours of circling over Australia, landing in the same place from where they left.[1]

Chalk it up to COVID-19. People were weary of being stuck at home. In response to months of going nowhere, they shelled out hundreds of dollars to—well, go nowhere.

Forgive my bluntness, but I'll keep my money in my pocket and my feet on the ground. Fly in circles? No, thank you. Fly toward a destination? That's better. And that's biblical.

Inherent in the pages of Scripture is this promise: we end up in a better place than where we began. We survive the winter times of life because we believe that a glorious springtime awaits us.

We survive the winter times of life because we believe that a glorious springtime awaits us.

This promise is buttressed by a quartet of convictions. They surface in the first chapter of the Bible's first book and thread their way through Scripture until the final page of the final book.

- We were made to reign.
- God has made and will keep his promises.
- Heaven has a time line.
- A golden era, the millennium, awaits God's children.

Four big ideas. They serve as pillars in the discussion of what's about to happen. Consider them the big rocks in the end-times jar around which the smaller pebbles settle.

Most of us are familiar with many of those smaller pebbles. When we think about the end times, several specific images and ideas surface in our minds. The seven years of chaos called the tribulation. The cruelty and charisma of the Antichrist. The jaw-dropping spectacle of Armageddon, that final battle long promised and long dreaded. These are the plot points that make end-times discussions so stimulating—scary as a serpent's fang and explosive as the Fourth of July.

We're going to explore those plot points. I promise. We're going to address the big events and answer the big questions.

But let's start with these four ideas—these four pillars. They will give us a solid foundation for understanding God's plans for the future. Flying in circles? No. We are headed to a far better place than where we started.

CHAPTER 2

It Looks Like Reign

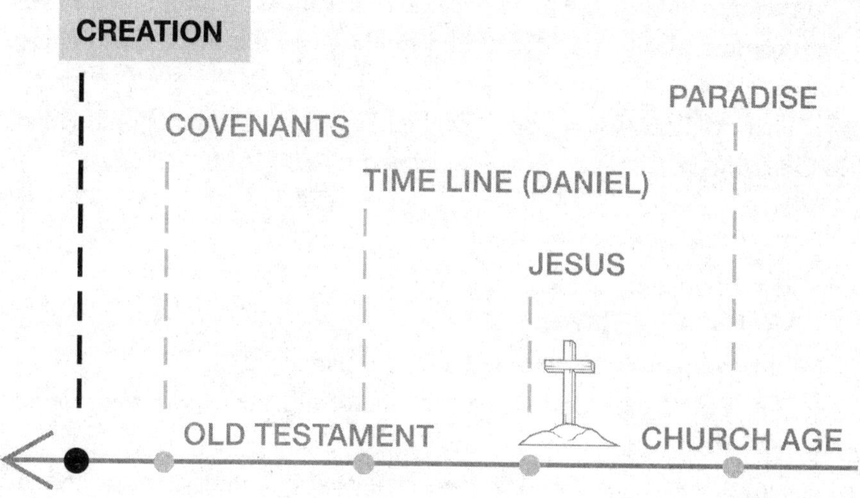

NO ONE HAS GREATER DREAMS for you than God does. The most insidious deception in human history is the lie that says, "God is against you." Nothing could be further from the truth. The one who came up with the very idea of you has plans for your future that are out of this world.

He unveiled them in history's most famous garden: Eden. Want to

God's designs for you and me were unveiled in Scripture's opening pages.

know what's coming next? Then consider what came first. God's designs for you and me were unveiled in Scripture's opening pages. Eschatology, the study of end things, begins with protology, the study of first things.

Your Destiny: Eden Fulfilled

Our story begins like this: "Then God said, 'Let us make human beings in our image, to be like us. They will reign over the fish in the sea, the birds in the sky, the livestock, all the wild animals on the earth, and the small animals that scurry along the ground'" (Gen. 1:26 NLT).

By this point God had created much. Stars sparkled at night. Clouds floated during the day. The air was sweet with the fragrance of flowers and the music of birds. Animals roamed the valleys and slept in the trees. But creation, albeit magnificent and mighty, was not made in the image of God.

That privilege was reserved for the likes of you and me. We are made in God's image.

Angels aren't.

Elephants aren't.

Jellyfish aren't.

My dog, Andy, isn't.

Only people are. Want to see how this happened?

"Then the LORD God formed the man from the dust of the ground" (Gen. 2:7 NLT).

Ladies, you've wondered why we men can be so messy. Simple, we are made from dust! Out of the soil of the garden, God shaped Adam's torso. He then carved out the two legs. He rounded the head and formed a nose. The same hand that flung stars in the heavens and scooped the floor for the ocean sculpted the first person.

Then, in an act that must have caused the angels to gasp, "he breathed the breath of life into the man's nostrils, and the man became a living person" (Gen. 2:7 NLT).

God exhaled. Adam inhaled. And for the first of what would be zillions of such occasions, lungs rose and emptied. Adam had life. But he had more than oxygen in him. He had God's breath in him. What a sterling, stunning creation he must have been. Unsullied by greed. Uncorrupted by hate. Untainted by guilt. Unacquainted with fear.

Adam was perfect. So perfect, in fact, that God gave him a job. "The LORD God placed the man in the Garden of Eden to tend and watch over it" (Gen. 2:15 NLT).

God commissioned Adam to care for creation, and God provided a partner to help him. What a delight to read God's announcement: "It is not good for the man to be alone" (Gen. 2:18 NLT).

For the first time God used the phrase "It is not good." When he saw the light, it was good. When he saw the land, it was good. Plants. Trees. Daytime. Nighttime. Good! Good! Good! Good!

But Adam? Alone? No companion? No partner? "Not good." So God brought animals and birds to Adam "to see what [the man] would call them. . . . But still there was no helper just right for him" (Gen. 2:19–20 NLT).

Adam exercised his role as overseer and assigned a name to each creature. He called the hippo a hippo, the rhino a rhino, the mosquito a mosquito. But the man could find no "helper just right for him" (v. 20 NLT).

And, men, aren't we glad? What if he'd chosen a warthog as a helper? But God had a special gift for Adam.

> So the LORD God caused the man to fall into a deep sleep. While the man slept, the LORD God took out one of the man's ribs and closed up the opening. Then the LORD God made a woman from the rib, and he brought her to the man.
>
> "At last!" the man exclaimed.
>
> "This one is bone from my bone,
>   and flesh from my flesh!
> She will be called 'woman,'
>   because she was taken from 'man.'"
>
> This explains why a man leaves his father and mother and is joined to his wife, and the two are united into one. (Gen. 2:21–24 NLT)

God put Adam to sleep (thereby forever sanctifying the act of a good nap), extracted a rib from Adam's side, and created the perfect partner. Eve, like the bone from which she was made, was created to remain closest to Adam's heart. Life was good.

> Then God said, ". . . Let them have dominion over the fish of the sea and over the birds of the heavens and over the livestock and over all the earth and over every creeping thing that creeps on the earth." (Gen. 1:26 ESV)

So many words to be highlighted. Where to begin? Maybe with the pronoun *them*. "Let *them* . . ." (emphasis mine). The man and woman would be partners. Equally cherished by God. Equally made in God's image.

Together they would "have *dominion* over the fish . . . the birds . . . the livestock . . ." (emphasis mine).

They would reign over creation, co-regents with God.

Yet, something happened. Do we oversee the sea? Rule over the livestock? Have dominion over creation? Far from it. We can hardly get fish to bite, much less obey. Some animals would sooner eat us than submit to us. We agree with the New Testament writer who observed, "When God put [Adam and Eve] in charge of everything, nothing was excluded. But we don't see it yet, don't see everything under human jurisdiction" (Heb. 2:8 MSG).

Indeed, we don't. Instead of ruling the world, we feel ruled by the world. We see creation in a state of corruption, eruption, and pollution. Heat waves. Wildfires. Hurricanes. Earthquakes. Famines. "The whole creation has been groaning as in the pains of childbirth right up to the present time" (Rom. 8:22). Something is awry. What's more, we don't see male and female behaving as partners, but often as rivals.

What happened?

Sin happened. Rebellion happened. Satan happened. Greed happened. A villain infiltrated the garden. He convinced the couple that the garden, resplendent and abundant, was inadequate. Eden was not enough for the couple. They wanted to be like God. And God, who knows what is best for creation, said, "No." He temporarily suspended the garden-of-Eden plan. But he did not cancel it. He did not abandon it.

He certainly did not abandon us. Just the opposite.

God's Decision: Eden Reclaimed

God set in motion a plan of redemption that includes promises, prophets, and miracles. He made a covenant with Abraham. He raised up Joseph in Egypt. He gave courage to David and strength to Esther.

But, still, the people sinned. The curse of self-centeredness was inescapable. Adam sinned first. We've each sinned since. It would take a perfect man and a perfect sacrifice to overcome it.

Enter Jesus Christ.

Scripture calls him the last Adam (1 Cor. 15:45–49). The two had much in common. Like Adam, Jesus had no earthly father. Like Adam, Jesus was given authority over creation. Like Adam, Jesus was tempted. Unlike Adam, Jesus never sinned.

We can thank the apostle Paul for this concise summary:

> Here it is in a nutshell: Just as one person did it wrong and got us in all this trouble with sin and death, another person did it right and got us out of it. But more than just getting us out of trouble, he got us into life! One man said no to God and put many people in the wrong; one man said yes to God and put many in the right. (Rom. 5:18–19 MSG)

Jesus succeeded where Adam failed. He did for us what rescuers did for a group of children lost in the Amazon jungle.

On May 1, 2023, a small aircraft with seven passengers crashed in one of the most remote parts of the world: the Amazon rainforest. The Cessna was flying from one small village to a slightly larger one, hundreds of miles south of Bogotá, Colombia.

Evidently, the single-engine prop failed in midair, causing a forced meeting with the dense canopy of trees and the jungle's unforgiving floor. All seven passengers were presumed dead. The odds of survival were minimal. The search area was a hundred miles long and twenty miles wide.

It took Colombian special forces more than two weeks, but they eventually located the crash site. When they did, they were saddened to find three of the seven passengers had perished upon impact but surprised to learn the other four—all children, all siblings ranging from ages thirteen years to eleven months—were nowhere to be found. Not on board and not around the crash site.

Colombia stepped up the rescue efforts. The government dispatched 150 soldiers, 40 volunteers, and several rescue dogs. Tiny clues of hope were found: a baby bottle here, small footprints there, used diapers. The children had been raised near the jungle. The older ones knew which plants and bugs to avoid. Even so, they were just kids. How could they still be alive?

Days turned into weeks, and desperation grew. Rescuers dropped boxes of food, water, even whistles into the jungle, hoping these would help sustain the children. But day after day ended in despair. After more than a month of effort, the search crew began to wonder if the children were purposely dodging their help.

Turns out that was the case.

More than once, rescuers were within fifty feet of the kids. The children didn't know if men had come to hurt or help, so they refused the ones who could save them.[1]

Might that story be a parable for humanity?

The overarching message of the Bible is God's relentless pursuit of his family. What he decreed in heaven is declared through creation. He will have his garden. He will share it with his children. Our names have been written into the grand narrative of God.

But what have we done in response? We have resisted the one who came to save us.

Adam and Eve did so. "When they heard the sound of God strolling in the garden in the evening breeze, the Man and his Wife hid in the trees of the garden, hid from God" (Gen. 3:8 MSG).

They hid from God! We've been hiding ever since. Adam and Eve covered themselves in fig leaves. We cover ourselves in work or status. They ducked into the trees. We hide in the foliage of denial, pride, or shame.

God, never easily put off, sought them out. He asked a question that has rung through the ages.

"God called to the Man: 'Where are you?'" (Gen. 3:9 MSG). This was not a question of geography. God knew their location. This was a question of the heart. "Where are you in relation to me? To my plan for your life?"

The question augured a divine rescue mission. God began sending message after message, miracle after miracle, mercy after mercy. He used patriarchs, matriarchs, prophets, and preachers. He's not beyond using a whale, a donkey, or a burning bush if that's what it takes to get our attention.

The Colombians displayed similar devotion. They came up with a plan. What could convince the children to come out of hiding? The team got creative. They lowered speakers into the jungle and turned up the volume so that a message could be heard over a mile in any direction. And then, this detail is key, they played an invitation recorded by the siblings' beloved grandmother telling them to "stay in one place, the rescue team is here to help."

On day number forty, all four children—emaciated, insect-bitten, weak, and most of all, afraid—were found. Their grandmother's voice called them out of the shadows.

They just needed a voice they could trust.

We did as well.

So, in heaven's finest act of love, God became human. Jesus Christ entered our jungle of hurt and heartache. He spoke with a voice we could trust and issued a message we dare not resist. *I've come to take you out of here.*

Not only did he talk to us; he died for us. It was necessary that he do so. Remember, God's garden is perfect. Yet God's children are anything but. When Jesus died on the cross, he died our death, paid our price, and took our place. He, the sinless, became a sinner so that we, the sinners, could be regarded as sinless.

God's dream has never changed. Consider his invitation:

> "Look! I have been standing at the door, and I am constantly knocking. If anyone hears me calling him and opens the door, I will come in and fellowship with him and he with me. I will let everyone who conquers sit beside me on my throne, just as I took my place with my Father on his throne when I had conquered." (Rev. 3:20–21 TLB)

God's storyline concludes with you, me, all his children living, ruling, dining, and serving with him in a perfect world. In the Bible's final book, these words are said to Jesus:

> "You were slain,
> and with your blood you purchased for God

> persons from every tribe and language and people and nation.
> You have made them to be a kingdom and priests to serve
> our God,
> and they will reign on the earth."
>
> (Rev. 5:9–10)

That's you! The final stop in your heavenly itinerary involves not just Eden but a position of authority in the garden. You will hold sway with God over creation.

Our authority in eternity is no small matter in Scripture. It is introduced in Genesis, confirmed in Revelation (22:5), and discussed by many, including Jesus himself! God's decree that we will reign with him is a fulfillment of his garden of Eden declaration. Jesus will share his dominion with us, his coheirs.

Pause and let that promise sink in. You will reign with Christ. There is so much banter these days about self-image and identity. For want of a good self-image, we drive fast cars, liposuction fat, join gangs, or wear tight (or baggy) jeans.

Yet, what better cure for a rotten self-image than the discovery of our eternal destiny! God is grooming us for a divine assignment. Jesus said, "I confer on you a kingdom, just as my Father conferred one on me, so that you may eat and drink at my table in my kingdom and sit on thrones" (Luke 22:29–30). You mean this much to God! His purpose and plan for you may begin in this life, but it won't be fully realized until the life to come.

The world can be so hard. We feel marginalized and sidelined. Society makes a big deal out of the rich and beautiful. Many of us are neither. Yet, all feelings of insignificance will melt the moment Jesus, King Jesus, crowns and commissions us. Exactly how will we serve? Where will we serve? And when will this all start?

Let's unpack those questions in the next few chapters. For now, embrace the big idea. Believe in the God who believes in you!

You aren't on a dead-end street. Your journey doesn't end with your final heartbeat. Your worth is not measured by the number of bucks in the bank or diplomas on your wall or followers on your socials or lovers in your bed or gadgets in your garage or tattoos on your skin. You are not here for possessions, power, or prestige.

You aren't on a dead-end street. Your journey doesn't end with your final heartbeat.

The story of Eden is not just the story about the first person but a picture of God's plan for each person. What God did for Adam he did for you. He formed you. He breathed life into you. And he destined you to serve him in a perfect place. Can you hear him? "I see something great in you. Would you accept my destiny for your life?"

Oh, I do pray you will.

If you've never said yes to Jesus, take a moment and do so. It's not complicated. Jesus has done the work. Just say to him something like this:

Jesus,

I am not perfect, for I have sinned.

But I believe in you. Save me, change me, forgive me.

I give you my life.

In Jesus' name I pray, amen.[2]

CHAPTER 3

Compelling Covenants

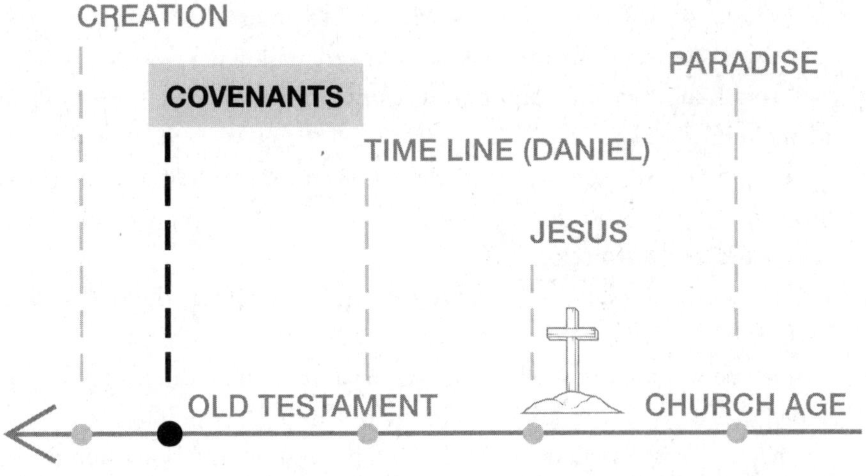

MY DAD MADE A BIG DEAL out of family vacations. Our holidays always consisted of a long road trip that began at our home in West Texas and ended up in a campground. Colorado and New Mexico were favorite destinations. He even drove us as far as Yellowstone National Park and the Grand Canyon.

Weeks before we left he would start planning the itinerary. He had no internet or GPS; he planned his trips the old-fashioned way: he used a map.

He traced out the journey with a highlighter. He circled the campgrounds and made notes of the highway numbers. Once he had his plans, he shared them with us.

My brother and I were just kids, single-digits in age and inexperienced in the ways of the road. So Dad would sit with us at the table, show us the map, and tell us what to expect.

"Boys, we leave next week for the Grand Canyon."

"Wow!"

"Let me tell you all the things we will do." Trout fishing. Tent camping. Marshmallow melting. Whitewater rafting.

My brother and I grew saucer-eyed. We had every reason to do so. When Dad said we would do something, we always did it. It was as good as done.

Having shared his route, he would also tell us what to expect along the way.

"When we drive through New Mexico, it's going to get windy."

"When we reach the mountains, your ears will pop."

"You'll know we are almost at the campground when you see snow on the mountain peaks."

Wouldn't you know it, his forecast was spot-on. The wind *did* blow. Our ears *did* pop. And the snowy peaks *were* the last thing we saw before we reached our destination.

He told us his plans and what to expect. Good fathers do that.

Our heavenly Father has done that.

Do you want to know what God has in store for humanity? Start in the garden of Eden. We find our end in the beginning. As pointed out in the last chapter, God revealed our destination in creation. But don't stop there. Next, get acquainted with his covenants.

A covenant is a contract, a treaty, an agreement, or alliance between two parties. It formally binds the two parties in a relationship with consequences for breaking or keeping the covenant. The covenant can be mutual or one-sided.

Our God is a covenant-making and covenant-keeping God. He does not lie. He *cannot* lie. "Your royal decrees cannot be changed" (Ps. 93:5 TLB). He can no more break a promise than you and I can swim the Pacific Ocean.

> God is not a human being, and he will not lie.
> He is not a human, and he does not change his mind.
> What he says he will do, he does.
> What he promises, he makes come true.
>
> (Num. 23:19 NCV)

God is not like us. We remake our decisions and reconsider our opinions. We are prone to make a promise only to break it due to unforeseen circumstances. Not God. He sees the end of history. His decrees are not his desire for the future. They are his description of the future.

He declared:

> "I am GOD, the only God you've had or ever will have—
> incomparable, irreplaceable—
> From the very beginning
> telling you what the ending will be,
> All along letting you in
> on what is going to happen,
> Assuring you, 'I'm in this for the long haul,
> I'll do exactly what I set out to do.'"
>
> (Isa. 46:9–10 MSG)

God's covenants serve like the autopilot feature on an airplane. A few years ago I decided to pursue a pilot's license. My wife, Denalyn, groaned at the thought. I take wrong turns when I drive a car. I stray off course on a walk through the neighborhood. Why, I can get lost between the bedroom and bathroom. What would I do on an airplane?

I tried to assuage her fears by describing the most amazing technology, the autopilot. Set the destination and the plane stays on course. It moves from waypoint to waypoint until it reaches the journey's end.

Turns out, I never had the opportunity to use one. Life got complicated, and I had to quit the lessons. But the effort wasn't a total waste. I found a wonderful way to illustrate God's covenants. He has set history on

God sees the end of history. His decrees are not his desire for the future. They are his description of the future.

autopilot. We are on a divine trajectory. That trajectory is governed by his promises. What God has set out to do, he will do.

Hence, a fundamental end-times question is, "What has God set out to do?" Resist the temptation to jump ahead to the more vibrant end-times discussions: the rapture, the tribulation, and the millennium. What happens in the latter days will make more sense once you know what God promised in the early days. We can stand on the foundation stones of God's compelling covenants.

Let's look at a few of them: one to Adam and Eve, a second to Abraham and his heirs, a third to David, and a final covenant to Jeremiah.[1]

God's Covenant with Adam and Eve

> Then God said, "Let us make human beings in our image and likeness. And let them rule over the fish in the sea and the birds in the sky, over the tame animals, over all the earth, and over all the small crawling animals on the earth." (Gen. 1:26 NCV)

God declared a shared dominion. He bequeathed upon his first couple an assignment. They would oversee, superintend, and exercise authority over the earth. Our first parents were placed in charge of real animals and real fish on real land in the real sea. The Hebrew term for *rule* is "have dominion" or "dominate."[2]

Adam and Eve fulfilled this promise—until they did not.

Their allegiance faltered, but did God's? Did he change his mind? Abandon his plan? No scripture indicates a shift in divine strategy. God's covenant was not written with easy-erase markers on a dry board, but by God's finger in stone. Remember: "What I have said, . . . that I will do" (Isa. 46:11).

Just as my father's itinerary guided his family, so God's Edenic covenant is leading us to a time in which God's perfected children will reign over a perfect earth. We will someday declare the words of Jeremiah: "The LORD has done what he planned; he has fulfilled his word, which he decreed long ago" (Lam. 2:17 NIV).

God also made a promise to Abraham and Abraham's heirs.

God's Covenant with Abraham

Two words serve as subheads for this covenant. *Seed* and *soil.*

First, God promised to bless the seed of Abraham (Abram) and bless the world through Abraham's seed.

> The LORD had said to Abram, "Go from your country, your people and your father's household to the land I will show you.
>
> "I will make you into a great nation,
> and I will bless you;
> I will make your name great,
> and you will be a blessing.
> I will bless those who bless you,
> and whoever curses you I will curse;
> and all peoples on earth
> will be blessed through you."
>
> (Gen. 12:1–3)

Why would God make such a covenant with Israel? Not because of anything Israel had to offer. Moses once reminded them: "GOD wasn't attracted to you and didn't choose you because you were big and important—the fact is, there was almost nothing to you. He did it out of sheer love, keeping the promise he made to your ancestors" (Deut. 7:7–8 MSG).

God chose Israel for the same reason he chose you and me: grace. Sheer, sovereign grace. He did not love them more than he loved other people groups of their day. He simply chose them as his billboard of grace. He wanted the other nations to see him through Israel so they would choose him to be their God as well.

"I will make you into a great nation. . . ." Has God not done exactly that? It's been over three and a half millennia since Abraham's death, yet look at us, still talking about Israel. We can't travel to the nations of the Babylonians or the Medes or Persians. The Roman and Greek empires are gone, but my passport bears multiple stamps from the nation of Israel.

Pharaoh attempted to eradicate them and failed. Haman sought to annihilate them and failed. Hitler sought to exterminate them and failed. Modern-day neighboring nations have sworn to erase Israel from the map. They will fail as well. There are Russian Jews, Polish Jews, American Jews, French Jews. Jews all over the world. God preserves their unique identity because he plans to use them in the end. God has blessed the seed of Abraham.

And has God not blessed the world through the seed of Abraham? Because of Abraham's seed, we have the prophets Isaiah, Ezekiel, and Daniel. We have King David and his psalms. We have Jerusalem and its history. But greatest by far we have a Savior, Jesus Christ. We have his Word, his church, and the blessed hope of his return.

God kept the seed promise. Can't we expect him to keep the soil promise as well?

> On that day the LORD made a covenant with Abram and said, "To your descendants I give this land, from the Wadi of Egypt to the great river, the Euphrates—the land of the Kenites, Kenizzites, Kadmonites, Hittites, Perizzites, Rephaites, Amorites, Canaanites, Girgashites and Jebusites." (Gen. 15:18–21)

Israel is the only nation in history to whom God has given land. This soil promise came with clear geographical boundaries. It encompasses all the land from the Mediterranean Sea on the western border to the Euphrates River on the east. The northern boundary extends a hundred miles north of Damascus (Ezek. 47:15–20), and the southern boundary is about one hundred miles south of Jerusalem.[3] This soil covenant includes modern-day Israel as well as parts of Egypt, Syria, Lebanon, and Iraq.[4]

God ratified this covenant with a ceremonial sacrifice of animals. In ancient times the two parties of an agreement would cut an animal in half and walk between the divided carcass. In a most dramatic moment, "when the sun went down and it was dark . . . there appeared a smoking oven and a burning torch that passed between those pieces. On the same day the LORD made a covenant with Abram, saying, 'To your descendants I have given this land'" (Gen. 15:17–18 NKJV).

Please note that Abraham did not reciprocate. The patriarch never walked between the pieces. This was a unilateral agreement made by God to Abraham and his seed. His covenant is untethered to performance. Elsewhere God assured, "I am as likely to reject my people Israel as I am to abolish the laws of nature!" (Jer. 31:36 NLT).

Has God fulfilled this soil covenant? Not entirely. The seed has been blessed, but the soil has yet to be completely given.

Will God keep this promise? Of course he will. He must! Charles Swindoll's paragraph on this point is starchy: "Why is the restoration of Israel so important? Because God's very reputation as a promise keeper is at stake! . . . It's as simple as this: If we cannot trust God to keep his promises to Israel, how can we trust Him to keep His promises to us? Never doubt it: God will do what He says He will do!"[5]

Amen!

He will also honor a guarantee he made to Israel's second-most-famous king.

God's Covenant with David

"Your house and your kingdom shall be established forever before you. Your throne shall be established forever" (2 Sam. 7:16 NKJV).

God declared that someone from the house of David would sit on David's throne and rule over his kingdom forever. About a thousand years later, the angel Gabriel quoted this covenant to a young Hebrew girl named Mary: "He will be great, and will be called the Son of the Highest, and the Lord God will give Him the throne of His father David. And He will reign over the house of Jacob forever, and of His kingdom there will be no end" (Luke 1:32–33 NKJV).

The pledge was clear:

- A future ruler (Jesus) will be called the "Son of the Highest."
- His throne will pass through Solomon to David's descendants.
- The King on the throne will rule over the nation of Israel.

For this to happen, Israel must exist as a nation. (It does.) David's descendant must be alive. (He is.) Jesus Christ must return to earth. (He will.) And he must bodily and literally sit on David's throne and reign over Israel.

God's plan for the end includes his fulfillment of this promise to David. At some point in the future, Jesus—the "Son of the Highest"—will rule over Israel from David's throne in Jerusalem.

God's Covenant with Jeremiah

"The days are coming," declares the LORD,
"when I will make a new covenant
with the people of Israel
and with the people of Judah. . . .

"I will put my law in their minds
and write it on their hearts.
I will be their God,
and they will be my people.
No longer will they teach their neighbor,
or say to one another, 'Know the LORD,'
because they will all know me,
from the least of them to the greatest,"
declares the LORD.
"For I will forgive their wickedness
and will remember their sins no more."

(Jer. 31:31, 33–34)

A Christian might read these words and conclude that God has already fulfilled this promise. He has put his instructions deep within us. His name is written on our hearts. He is our God. We are his people. He has forgiven our wickedness. He will never remember our sins. Hallelujah! This covenant has been honored!

Or has it? Look again. Who are the two parties to this agreement? One is God. And God made a unilateral, unconditional covenant, not with the church but with Israel. "The days are coming," declares the LORD, "when

I will make a new covenant with *the people of Israel and with the people of Judah*" (Jer. 31:31, emphasis mine).

In a parallel prophecy, God affirmed:

> "I will take you [Israel] out of the nations . . . and bring you back into your own land. . . . I will give you a new heart and put a new spirit in you. . . . And I will put my Spirit in you and move you to follow my decrees and be careful to keep my laws. Then you will live in the land I gave your ancestors; you will be my people, and I will be your God." (Ezek. 36:24, 26–28)

What a stunning, surprising, and compelling covenant! It envisions a return and a revival among the Jews. They will resettle their homeland and revive their allegiance to the God of Abraham.

As a reminder, the regathering is already in full force. Since 1948 more than three million Jews have made *aliyah*, a move to the historic homeland of the people of Israel.[6] The population of that nation is projected to reach twenty million by 2065.[7]

But what of the spiritual revival? It's coming. In upcoming chapters we will discuss the 144,000 Jewish evangelists who will go forth into the world, resulting in a "great multitude which no one could number, of all nations, tribes, peoples, and tongues, standing before the throne and before the Lamb, clothed with white robes, with palm branches in their hands, and crying out with a loud voice, saying, 'Salvation belongs to our God who sits on the throne, and to the Lamb'" (Rev. 7:9–10 NKJV).

Our end-time vision would be lacking if it did not include this migration of Jews to their native land and the revival of the Jews toward their Messiah.

Let's review. God's covenants include a promise to

- Adam and Eve—reign and rule
- Abraham—seed and soil
- David—a forever throne and a forever King
- Jeremiah—return and revival of the Jews

Be assured, God is at work. His plans are proceeding at the right pace, in the right places, and according to his will. What he has said he will do,

Be assured, God is at work. His plans are proceeding at the right pace, in the right places, and according to his will.

he will do. In the meantime lay hold of these great and precious promises. They are governing principles for the unfolding of history.

When our daughters were young, I followed my dad's example and took them on many road trips. Like most parents, Denalyn and I liked to get a jump on the traffic by leaving before the sun was up.

On the eve of our departure, I'd tell my daughters what was about to happen. "You will fall asleep in your bed. But early tomorrow, while you are still sleeping, I will carry you to the car, cover you with a blanket, and buckle you in your seat. By the time you wake up, we will be on the road."

I told them in advance what would happen. Consequently, when it happened, they did not panic. They didn't awaken, see their surroundings, and scream, "I've been kidnapped!"

No, they relaxed and watched the road go by. Their father had told them what to expect.

Our Father has done the same. So, as his promises are being fulfilled, we have no need to fear. We can relax, knowing that our Father has the wheel.

CHAPTER 4

God's Plan for the Ages

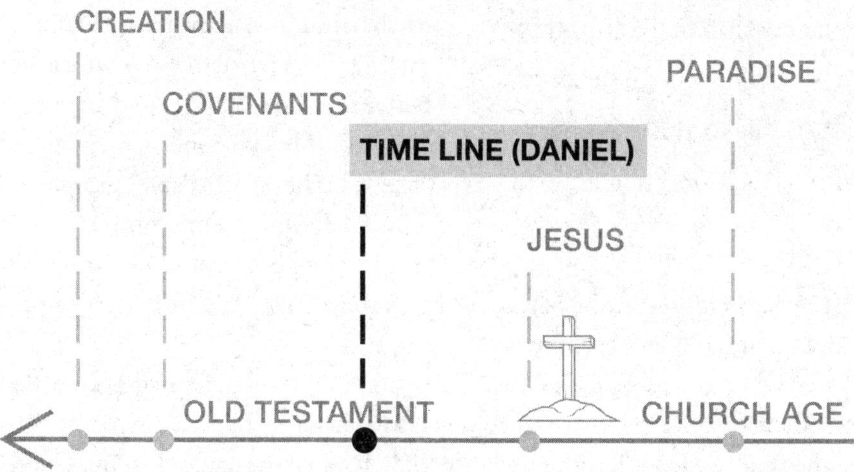

I'D LIKE TO SHAKE THE HAND of the person who put the little plane in the big plane. Perhaps you've seen it? Perhaps you've done what I've done—dozed off on a flight and awakened to wonder, "Where in the world are we?" "How long before we land?" "How far have we gone?"

For much of my traveling life, I had no answer. I could ask the attendants, but they seemed busy. I could look out the window for reference points, but either the sky was dark or cloudy or we were too high to determine anything. I could ask the pilot, but passengers who knock on the cockpit door get in trouble.

Then came the little plane inside the big plane. You can look at the screen on the seat in front of you and see a dotted line that begins at the city of origin and ends at the destination—and there, somewhere on the route, is the tiny replica of the very flight you are on.

"Oh," you tell yourself. "There we are. We're making good progress."

Or, "We've got a long way to go."

Or, "We are flying over the Alps."

Why, one time I looked intently at the image and spotted a window of the tiny plane and saw myself! I had a spot on my shirt!

I'm grateful for the little plane inside the big plane.

Did you know God has provided something similar for us? Specifically, he has given us a time line. History is not an endless succession of meaningless circles but an ordered, orchestrated movement toward God's eternal goal.

History is not an endless succession of meaningless circles but an ordered, orchestrated movement toward God's eternal goal.

One of the earliest references to the time line appears in Daniel 9 during a surprising conversation between God's prophet and the angel Gabriel. That vision is often called "the backbone of Bible prophecy." This foretelling, while powerful, can appear complicated and requires careful examination. Yet the harvest is worth the tilling. If you are ready to turn over some soil, let's get to work.

By the time Daniel received the vision in question, he had been exiled in Babylonia for nearly seventy years. He was a Hebrew lad when he was taken captive from Jerusalem in 605 BC. Toward the end of his life, Daniel called on God to forgive the Jewish people and return them to their homeland. "While I was saying these things in my prayer to the Lord, my God, confessing my sins and the sins of the people of Israel and praying for God's holy hill, Gabriel came to me" (Dan. 9:20–21 NCV).

Gabriel, the same angel who announced the arrival of John the Baptist and Jesus Christ approximately five hundred years later, spoke to Daniel in Babylon. He declared three prophecies.

The Jews Will Be Blessed

> "God has ordered four hundred ninety years for your people and your holy city for these reasons: to stop people from turning against God; to put an end to sin; to take away evil; to bring in goodness that continues forever; to bring about the vision and prophecy; and to appoint a most holy place." (Dan. 9:24 NCV)

Gabriel gave Daniel insider information on something that would occur at the end of 490 years. He limited this prophecy to "your people and your holy city." Meaning Daniel, himself a Jewish man, was told the future state of the capital city and his kin. After 490 years the Jewish people would

- stop turning against God,
- see an end to sin,
- witness evil taken away,
- welcome a goodness that continues forever, and
- establish a holy place (a temple).

Have these decrees been fulfilled? Do Jews stay away from sin? Has the temple in Jerusalem been rededicated? No and no and no. These events have yet to occur. Obviously, the angel was describing a spectacular era in the future.

When will this period begin? At the conclusion of *a total* of 490 years. Just about the time we pull out our calculators and calendars to measure 490 years from the day of Daniel's prayer, Gabriel gave prophecy number two.

The Messiah Is on the Way

> "A command will come to rebuild Jerusalem. The time from this command until the appointed leader comes will be forty-nine years and four hundred thirty-four years." (Dan. 9:25 NCV)

The Hebrew term for "appointed leader" means *Messiah*. Gabriel was talking about Jesus the Christ! This was a monumental announcement.

The angel mentioned two blocks of time—49 years and 434 years, for a total of 483 years.

But, Max, I thought Gabriel was talking about 490 years? What about the remaining seven?

Great question. We will answer it soon.

When does the countdown for the 483 years begin? With the command to rebuild Jerusalem. Specifically, "Jerusalem will be rebuilt with streets and a trench filled with water around it, but it will be built in times of trouble" (v. 25 NCV). When was a command issued to rebuild the capital? And when was the city rebuilt "with streets and a trench in times of trouble"? How quickly can your fingers flip the pages of your Bible to the book of Nehemiah?

Nehemiah was a high-ranking exiled Jewish ruler who lived some 130 years after Daniel received this prophecy. He made a request to Artaxerxes to rebuild Jerusalem. The king agreed to permit and fund the project. According to Nehemiah 2:1, the command was given in April of 444 BC.

We have a starting point! Flip the yearly calendar 483 times, beginning in 444 BC, and where do you land in history?

This question became the obsession of Sir Robert Anderson. In the late 1800s he was the chief of Scotland Yard, an English lawyer, and a serious student of the book of Daniel. He set out to determine the end date of the 483 years. This task was not as easy as one might assume. The Hebrew calendar is not like our calendar. It has 360 days instead of 365 and leap months instead of leap years. Then there was the tricky transition from BC to AD. Even so, his calculations led him to a most significant finding.[1]

Anderson determined that the 483rd year occurred during the Passover of AD 33; specifically on April 6, the very year and day that Jesus rode into Jerusalem on the back of a donkey.[2] Our Savior fulfilled a prophecy that dated back 483 years![3]

It's no wonder that the multitudes were out in droves to welcome Jesus with palm leaves. They had read the prophecy of Daniel!* They knew they were living in the days of fulfilled promise. The air was flush with Messianic expectation.

---

* Please see Bonus Material from Max, p. 188, for additional information on response to Daniel's prophecy.

Gabriel's forecast was so precise that Jesus had harsh words for those who missed it. "When He approached Jerusalem, He saw the city and wept over it, saying, 'If you had known on *this day*, even you, the conditions for peace! But now they have been hidden from your eyes. . . . you did not recognize *the time* of your visitation" (Luke 19:41, 42, 44 NASB, emphasis mine).

Jesus criticized his antagonists because the "day" and "time" were theirs to expect, yet they were not paying attention. He had previously dispatched an angel to his beloved prophet Daniel. He issued his arrival date 483 years in advance. Yet, "his own did not receive him" (John 1:11). They refused to recognize him as their Messiah. Instead of crowning him as king, they killed him as a criminal.

Gabriel told Daniel this would happen. Remember, the angel spoke of two blocks of time: 49 years and 434 years. It took 49 years to rebuild Jerusalem. What about the 434 years?

"After the four hundred thirty-four years the appointed leader will be killed; he will have nothing" (Dan. 9:26 NCV). True to Gabriel's presage, Jesus was killed. It appeared he had nothing. No followers. No kingdom. He was dead and buried in a borrowed grave. What's more, the city of Jerusalem soon fell under attack from the Romans. Gabriel augured that event this way: "The people of the leader who is to come will destroy the city and the holy place. The end of the city will come like a flood, and war will continue until the end. God has ordered that place to be completely destroyed" (v. 26 NCV).

This gloomy prophecy was fulfilled on August 6, AD 70. Titus of Rome destroyed Jerusalem, killed a million Jews, and tore the temple apart stone by stone.[4]

Do you not find this to be a stunning text?

Studying it led Leopold Kahn, a former rabbi, to become a Christian.[5]

Sir Isaac Newton said we could stake the truth of Christianity on this prophecy alone.[6]

Dr. Bill Creasy, a distinguished professor at UCLA, called this portent "one of the most extraordinary examples of long-range, specific prophecy in the Bible."[7]

Dr. Mark Hitchcock, author of a five-hundred-page comprehensive book on end times, wrote: "The precision of this prophecy is staggering! I call it the greatest prophecy ever given. It stands as a monumental proof of the inspiration of the Bible."[8]

Yet, the observant person has a question. Gabriel foretold 490 years. He explained the first 483 and then stopped. What about the remaining seven?

Tough Times Are Coming

> "That leader will make firm an agreement with many people for seven years. He will stop the offerings and sacrifices after three and one-half years. A destroyer will do blasphemous things until the ordered end comes to the destroyed city." (Dan. 9:27 NCV)

Wait a second. Who is "that leader"? What is this seven-year agreement? How can the ruler stop sacrifices after three and a half years if the temple has been destroyed and, consequently, the temple sacrifices have been discontinued? What just happened?

Here is what many other end-times students and I think: God stopped the 490-year countdown clock at year number 483. When the Jews rejected their Messiah, God pressed pause. There is a gap of time between years 483 and 484—a hiatus between the events described in Daniel 9:26 and 27.

Why would I believe this? Because the events described in verse 27 have not happened. We have yet to see the moment in which offerings and sacrifices in the temple are disallowed. There is no temple currently. This is a yet-to-be-fulfilled prophecy that alludes to the final 7 years of the 490 years. That period will involve a rebuilt temple,* its defilement, a treaty, and an evil despot. Maybe you've heard of him.

The Antichrist. He is the warmonger of the end times, the enemy of God, and the nemesis of the Jews. The phrase "leader who is to come" (Dan. 9:26 NCV) refers to him. He will be the pawn of Satan in a final, fatal, and futile attempt to overthrow the kingdom of God. He will enter a pact with the state of Israel. Under the terms of this treaty, Israel will either continue or begin the construction of the temple.

At first the Jews will be delighted with their new friend. The world

* Please see Bonus Material from Max, p. 188, for information on the Temple Mount.

will sigh with relief at the appearance of peace in the Middle East. Yet, midway through the seven-year treaty, the Antichrist's true nature will be disclosed. He will tear up the agreement and seize the rebuilt temple. He will install his image and demand universal worship. He will impose his will on the world (Rev. 13:1–18).

Jesus Christ spoke of this moment: "So when you see standing in the holy place 'the abomination that causes desolation,' spoken of through the prophet Daniel—let the reader understand—then let those who are in Judea flee to the mountains" (Matt. 24:15–16).

This seven-year season of global struggle is often called the tribulation. God will use this time of testing to purge and purify the nation of Israel and to populate the new kingdom with people of faith. He will then declare his final judgment against the would-be world leader. Christ will come a second time to establish a kingdom. Every eye will see him (Zech. 14:3–4; Rev. 1:7). Every knee will bow before him. And the Son of Man will rule from Jerusalem. At that point the 490 years will be completed, and the millennium, the golden age, will begin.

Is your head spinning?

Let's pause and get our bearings. Here is the chronology:

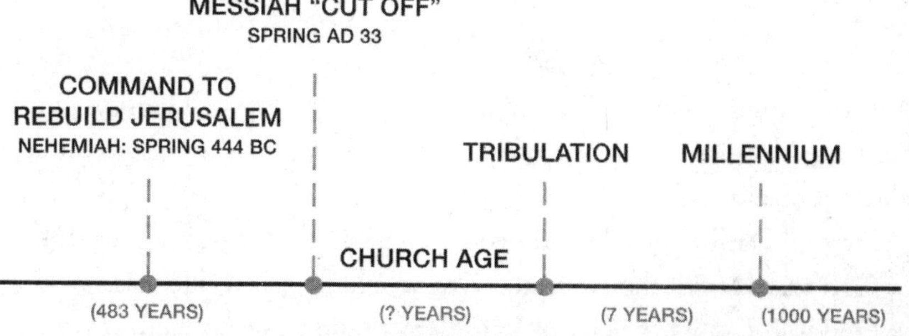

Do you see where we are on this time line? We live in "the church age" or "the age of grace," which is the parenthetical period that sits between the Messiah and the tribulation.

You might be wondering, *Why the gap? Why would God create this separate phase for the church age?*

Here's the answer: it's a *musterion*. That's the Greek word Paul used to describe this parenthetical period. A mystery. A secret God kept hidden in his heart. Between the death of Christ and the final seven years of human history as we know it, God added a new age.

> In reading this, then, you will be able to understand my insight into the mystery of Christ, which was not made known to people in other generations as it has now been revealed by the Spirit to God's holy apostles and prophets. This mystery is that through the gospel the Gentiles are heirs together with Israel, members together of one body, and sharers together in the promise in Christ Jesus. (Eph. 3:4–6)

God inserted the church into history. The church age features a new society formed by Jew and Gentile, male, female, slave, free. You, other believers, and I find ourselves somewhere in this parenthetic era. To be clear, the final seven years are still to come. But they will be poisoned by history's most evil despot.

The prophecy in Daniel 9 is so vital. It speaks of God's time line for history. It includes a precise prophecy about the Messiah and an early reference to the Antichrist and the remaining seven years on God's prophetic calendar. Before we move forward on that time line, let's catch our breath and make three observations.

You Can Trust Bible Prophecy

I read about a psychic shop that went out of business. The sign on the door read: "Closed due to unforeseen circumstances." God has no unforeseen circumstances.

He told Daniel the Messiah would come after 483 years. Jesus did.

God told Daniel the Anointed One would be killed. He was.

God told Daniel the city of Jerusalem would be devastated. It was.

These and dozens of other prophecies compel us to take God at his word. The same pages that foretell prophecies down to the exact date are the pages that describe God's love and devotion for you. You can trust God's word.

The same pages that foretell prophecies down to the exact date are the pages that describe God's love and devotion for you. You can trust God's word.

You Can Be Prepared

Hard times are coming. The Antichrist, the tribulation, the abomination that causes desolation—these are foreboding events. But if you are in Christ, you won't have to experience them. God will come for his church before the dark days begin. That event is commonly called the rapture. Jesus, with the power of a king and the kindness of a savior, will extract his children prior to the seven years of evil. (We will dedicate chapter 7 to unpacking this exciting event in greater detail.)

Will you be like those who missed the time stamp of Jesus in his day and refused to recognize him as Messiah? Or will you be ready for the rescue?

You Can Have Security About the Ultimate Victory

Some years ago I attended a San Antonio Spurs basketball game. It was the final game of the regular season, and it was unique because it did not matter. The Spurs had already won their division. They had already clinched the top seed in the playoffs. The game had no bearing on their standings. Whether they won or lost did not matter. Since they had already won the division, they could not lose, even if they lost.

In these last days show up, play hard, and be happy. After all, the victory is secure.

The game was of little or no interest to the sports world. But it intrigued this preacher. I saw a sermon illustration waiting to happen. Christians occupy the same spot that the Spurs did. According to the Bible, we've already won. According to prophecy, victory is secure. According to the message of grace and the death of Christ on the cross, no one can snatch us from our Father's hand.

Yet, we still have a few contests before the final conquest. So how do we behave in the meantime?

The Spurs were a good example. I've never seen a team enjoy a game more than they did that night. They were relaxed, confident, and happy. Because they were, they won the game.

That's our strategy. Let's keep our eyes on the little plane inside the big plane. In these last days show up, play hard, and be happy. After all, the victory is secure.

CHAPTER 5

Millenni-what?

WE SING ABOUT IT EVERY CHRISTMAS. We may not know that we do, but we do. The hard-hearted sing about it. The secular cynical sing about it. The barely sober sing about it. We all sing about the millennium.

It might surprise you to know that when Isaac Watts wrote "Joy to the World," he wasn't writing a Christmas carol.[1] He was reflecting on Psalm 98, a text that celebrates the upcoming thousand-year earthly reign of Jesus. During this golden age, Jesus will rule the world *in truth and grace.* He will *make the nations prove the wonders of His love.* He will make His blessings *flow as far as the curse is found.*

Isaac Watts was one of many students of Scripture who look forward to an era of unprecedented peace and prosperity: an age during which Jesus will reign from a physical throne in a geographical Jerusalem and, for an extended period, the world will rest.

Not all students of Scripture agree with Watts. There are many God-fearing, Christ-seeking, heaven-bound men and women who see the Bible's references to the thousand-year reign as a symbol, a metaphor. The discussion is a rigorous one.

Christians agree on three essentials:

1. The visible return of Jesus Christ
2. The bodily resurrection of the dead
3. The final judgment of all people

These fundamental truths form the foundation of the Christian hope regarding the end times. They comprise and create the common ground upon which we can serve together, enjoy fellowship, and worship Jesus. While there is robust discussion regarding details of what's about to happen, we cannot let different interpretations threaten our common bond. We can be decisive but never divisive.

Christ is coming. The dead will be living. And everything will be set right.

Christ is coming. The dead will be living. And everything will be set right.

Amen!

Many Christians feel no need for further discussion. (In fact, just mention the topic of end times, and some run for the hills.) Others of us, however, are curious. We want to know what happens next. Foundational to this question is a more focused query: How are we to interpret the golden age described by the prophet John?

> Then I saw an angel coming down from heaven with the key to the bottomless pit and a heavy chain in his hand. He seized the dragon—that old serpent, who is the devil, Satan—and bound him in chains for a thousand years. The angel threw him into the bottomless pit, which he then shut and locked so Satan could not deceive the nations anymore until the thousand years were finished. Afterward he must be released for a little while.
>
> Then I saw thrones, and the people sitting on them had been given the authority to judge. And I saw the souls of those who had been beheaded for their testimony about Jesus and for proclaiming the word of God. They had not worshiped the beast or his statue, nor accepted his mark on their foreheads or their hands. They all came to life again, and they reigned with Christ for a thousand years.
>
> This is the first resurrection. (The rest of the dead did not come

> back to life until the thousand years had ended.) Blessed and holy are those who share in the first resurrection. For them the second death holds no power, but they will be priests of God and of Christ and will reign with him a thousand years. (Rev. 20:1–6 NLT)

John spoke as one transported into a different realm, like a man lifted from earth and dropped into a future event. He witnessed an angel slap handcuffs on the devil and throw him into a pit. He spoke of the dead coming to life and the celebration of saints.

Students of the Bible interpret this text in different ways.

Some see it as figurative (nonliteral) language and believe we are in the millennium now. They believe the kingdom of God began with the first coming of Jesus and will be consummated by his second coming. This view has come to be called *amillennialism*.

Others believe the kingdom of God will gradually progress into a time of worldwide peace that will end with the second coming of Jesus. The reference to a thousand years is seen as symbolic, simply describing a long period of time. This view is often described as *postmillennialism* because it identifies Jesus' second coming as occurring after (post) the millennium.

Still others interpret Revelation 20 as describing a literal thousand-year period in which Satan will be bound and Christ will be king. Most call this *premillennialism* because it refers to Jesus' second coming occurring before (pre) the millennium.[2]

What Difference Does It Make?

Does it matter what view a person takes? Regarding salvation, not one bit. We are saved by grace through faith in Jesus, not by cracking the code of millennialism.

Our answer does, however, shape the way we see end-time events. Do you believe the millennium is symbolic, figurative language? Then your time line is simple. Christ will return in judgment. The saved will be saved. The lost souls will be condemned, and our eternal state will begin.

Do you hold to a more literal interpretation of Revelation 20? If so,

> We are saved by grace through faith in Jesus, not by cracking the code of millennialism.

then you likely anticipate other dramatic moments: A rapture of the church into the presence of Christ. A time of severe tribulation on the earth. The triumphant return of Jesus from heaven. A thousand-year reset of nature and humankind.

Consider this metaphor: Imagine you are remodeling a century-old house. It has fallen into disrepair, and you are resolved to restore it to its original state. In the process of clearing out the rubble, you discover a stone fireplace. If it was a part of the initial design, you want to keep it. If added later, you want to remove it.

In our "what happens next" discussion, we face a similar decision. If the millennium is a part of God's original blueprint, let's frame our view of the last days around it. If not, if it was added later or never intended, then it can be disregarded. For that reason we need to discuss the *possibility* of the millennium at this juncture. We will address the *purpose* of the millennium in chapter 13.

So, will we experience a one-thousand-year reign with Jesus?

My answer is yes. Jesus will someday rule from the physical city of Jerusalem. The earth will be restored to its garden-of-Eden splendor, and we will walk on a perfect planet in perfected bodies. This interpretation is in line with the premillennial position.

What leads me to that conclusion? Interesting question. I never had a premillennial pastor or professor. The seminary I attended taught that the millennial kingdom is the current age. Yet as I studied Scripture for myself, a shift in my thinking took place. The reasons for that shift can be listed in an acrostic, P.O.W.E.R.

Promises Yet Unfulfilled

A millennial kingdom provides an opportunity for God's covenants to be honored. You might recall we discussed these covenants earlier. Here is a quick review.

The earliest covenant is found in the earliest words God spoke about humankind. "Be fruitful and multiply; fill the earth and subdue it" (Gen. 1:28 NKJV). This was our initial assignment: "Have dominion over the fish of the sea, over the birds of the air, and over the cattle, over all the earth and over every creeping thing that creeps on the earth" (Gen. 1:26 NKJV).

God gave instructions for us to "subdue" creation. The realm of this creation is "on the earth" (not heaven). Adam and Eve were created to oversee it. With the serpent came temptation. With temptation came rebellion. With rebellion came the fall. Consequently, humanity has fallen from its intended position as ruler of the earth.

Does our failure impact God's plan? Will he forsake it? Amend his covenant? No. He has decreed a future reign of Christ on earth in which we will be "priests of God and of Christ and will reign with him for a thousand years" (Rev. 20:6). We will do for a millennium what Adam and Eve did for a short while. We will rule in God's immaculate garden.

This unfulfilled covenant remains between God and humanity, and it will be realized.

What's more, unfulfilled covenants remain between God and Israel (Gen. 12:1–3 and 15:18). God promised Israel a specific piece of land: "to your descendants I give this land" (Gen. 15:18 RSV). The land includes the modern-day nation of Israel plus parts of modern-day Egypt, Syria, Lebanon, and Iraq (15:18–21). Though the Israelites inherited this land, they have yet to fully occupy it. This covenant was not fulfilled in the past and is not being fulfilled in the present. So shouldn't we expect it to be fulfilled in the future?

God also made a specific covenant with David that one of David's descendants would sit on David's throne and reign over his kingdom forever (2 Sam. 7:12–16). This pledge was specifically applied to Jesus when he was born: "the Lord God will give [Jesus] the throne of his father David" (Luke 1:32). Jesus is certainly ruling from heaven in the current age. But the promise made to David requires that Jesus sit on *David's throne* and rule over *David's kingdom*, the nation of Israel.

The millennial kingdom allows for this to occur.

We can add to this list of promises a collection of prophecies that fit neither the present age nor our heavenly state. Here is an example:

> "No longer will babies die when only a few days old.
> No longer will adults die before they have lived a full life.

> No longer will people be considered old at one hundred!
> Only the cursed will die that young!"
>
> (Isa. 65:20 NLT).

Isaiah foresaw an era in which newborns won't die and lifespans will stretch into centuries. This is far different from the present age, but it's also an inaccurate description of our eternal state when death shall be discontinued. Apparently heaven's itinerary includes a stage in history that is far greater than the status quo but far less than our final home. The millennium fits this description.

Other prophecies portend a unique chapter in humanity. Most notably:

> In that day the wolf and the lamb will live together;
> the leopard will lie down with the baby goat.
> The calf and the yearling will be safe with the lion,
> and a little child will lead them all.
>
> (Isa. 11:6 NLT)

Can you imagine such a renewal of nature? A time in which all animals and humans will coexist in peace? Sounds like heaven. But then we read the next passage:

> In that day the heir to David's throne
> will be a banner of salvation to all the world.
> The nations will rally to him,
> and the land where he lives will be a glorious place.
> In that day the Lord will reach out his hand a second time
> to bring back the remnant of his people—
> those who remain in Assyria and northern Egypt;
> in southern Egypt, Ethiopia, and Elam;
> in Babylonia, Hamath, and all the distant coastlands.
>
> (vv. 10–11 NLT)

These verses look forward to the same prophetic period, but it does not appear that the eternal state has begun during that period. Some people are still seeking salvation. The "nations will rally" and the Lord will reach out.

Yet the reversal of nature is not like anything we will see in this present age. Might this describe the millennium?[3]

Such a kingdom allows time and space for God's promises to be fulfilled. It also foresees the . . .

Overthrow of Satan

In John's vision, "[The angel] seized the dragon—that old serpent, who is the devil, Satan—and bound him in chains for a thousand years. The angel threw him into the bottomless pit, which he then shut and locked so Satan could not deceive the nations anymore until the thousand years were finished" (Rev. 20:2–3 NLT).

Satan is a fallen, embittered, and evil angel. He wreaks havoc on earth and leaves devastation in his wake. Every war, worry, and weary soul can be blamed on him. Hence, to imagine Satan bound, locked away from humanity—what an appealing thought!

Has this incarceration occurred? Has Satan been removed from the earth and locked away? Has he been taken hold of, bound, [thrown] into the abyss, and the abyss shut and sealed over him (Rev. 20:2–3 NASB)?

As far as I can tell, he is still the "ruler of this world" (John 12:31; 14:30 NASB), "the god of this world" (2 Cor. 4:4 NASB), "the commander of the powers in the unseen world" (Eph. 2:2 NLT), and a "roaring lion, looking for someone to devour" (1 Peter 5:8 GNT). Satan's incarceration is a yet-to-be event.

A more literal interpretation of Revelation 20 squares with the reality of the devil's upcoming demise. In fact, a more literal reading of Scripture is another reason to affirm the millennium.

Word-for-Word Interpretation

I wrote this phrase on the page in my Bible that precedes the book of Revelation: "When the plain sense of Scripture makes common sense, we will seek no other sense." I don't know who first set forth that rule, but I like it. The plainest reading of Revelation 20 is a literal thousand-year reign. John mentions it six times in seven verses:

1. Satan is bound "for a thousand years" (v. 2).
2. Satan could not deceive "until the thousand years were ended" (v. 3).

3. Saints "reigned with Christ a thousand years" (v. 4).
4. "The rest of the dead did not come to life until the thousand years were ended" (v. 5).
5. The saved "will reign with [Christ] for a thousand years" (v. 6).
6. The thousand years will come to an end (v. 7).

Why not take John's number literally?

Daniel would have. Recall that he was a prophet in the seventh century BC. Toward the end of his life, Daniel offered a prayer that occupies half of the ninth chapter of his book and deserves a spot on the list of the great prayers of the Bible. Daniel called on God to forgive the Jewish people and return them to Jerusalem.

What prompted the prayer? He was reading the prophecy of Jeremiah, a prophet from the prior generation: "This whole country will become a desolate wasteland, and these nations will serve the king of Babylon seventy years" (Jer. 25:11).

This is a prophet reading a prophet, thereby teaching us how to read prophecy. At the time Daniel read Jeremiah's prediction, sixty-seven years of captivity had passed. So with the seventy years coming to an end, he prayed for God to keep his promise. Daniel didn't assume seventy was a symbolic number. He didn't define seventy as a metaphorical phrase for an undisclosed number of years. When he read the phrase "seventy years," he assumed it meant seventy literal years.

For that reason, unless there is a clear reason to do otherwise, I lean literal. If prophecy speaks of seventy years, I assume seventy years. In the book of Revelation, John promised a thousand-year reign of Christ. I think Daniel would have taken the number at face value.

The first-century Christians appeared to have done so. Their conviction is another reason to consider a literal millennium to come.

Early Church Fathers

For the first three hundred years of church history, almost all its leaders were premillennial.[4] Most significant among them was Papias (AD 60–130), the Bishop of Hierapolis, who was a disciple of none other than the apostle John.[5] If a student of the author of Revelation ascribed to a literal understanding of the millennium in Revelation 20, that's a compelling argument to do the same.

The list of early adherents to the literal reign of Christ also includes Irenaeus (c. 120–202) and Tertullian (160–230). Justin Martyr, who died in AD 165, wrote, "But I and others, who are right-minded Christians on all points, are assured that there will be a resurrection of the dead, and a thousand years in Jerusalem, which will then be built, adorned, and enlarged, [as] the prophets Ezekiel and Isaiah and others declare."[6]

The church fathers embraced the promise of an earthly reign of Jesus on earth. The evidence of history is compelling.

So is the teaching of . . .

Resurrections in Revelation

John foresaw two of those resurrections:

> Then I saw thrones, and the people sitting on them had been given the authority to judge. And I saw the souls of those who had been beheaded for their testimony about Jesus and for proclaiming the word of God. They had not worshiped the beast or his statue, nor accepted his mark on their foreheads or their hands. They all came to life again, and they reigned with Christ for a thousand years.
>
> This is the first resurrection. (The rest of the dead did not come back to life until the thousand years had ended.) (Rev. 20:4–5 NLT)

John is referring to the tribulation—the seven years of trouble, which we will soon discuss. The tribulation will be a season of struggle for all people, especially those who resist Satan. Only those who take his mark on their foreheads or hands will buy and sell.[7] Multitudes will refuse to kneel before the devil's goons. They will be killed for their beliefs and come to life again and reign with Christ for a thousand years. This is the first resurrection. John is careful to point out: "The rest of the dead did not come back to life until the thousand years had ended" (v. 5).

Two resurrections: one for the redeemed and one for the rebels. One at the beginning of the millennium, one at the end. If there is no millennium, how can there be two resurrections?

P.O.W.E.R.

As I mentioned earlier, I have not always interpreted Scripture to teach a literal millennial kingdom to come. Professors and preachers to whom I owe my understanding of salvation, grace, and ultimate victory influenced me to read prophecies about the thousand years through a figurative lens. Of course, I still respect those teachers and understand their point of view.

But:

Promises yet unfulfilled,
Overthrow of Satan,
Word-for-word interpretation,
Early church fathers, and
Resurrections in Revelation
convince me that Christ will reign on the earth in P.O.W.E.R.

Just moments prior to his ascension into heaven, the followers of Christ inquired, "Lord, will You at this time restore the kingdom to Israel?" (Acts 1:6 NKJV).

Many scholars give the apostles a bad rap for this inquiry. They accuse them of misinterpretation, thinking they had one thing in mind when they talked about the "kingdom"—specifically, a literal kingdom headquartered in Israel in which Christ would reign as King—while Jesus was only interested in something more symbolic. If that's the case, we would expect Jesus to correct them and adjust their thinking.

We listen for the Master's kind rebuke, but it doesn't come. He simply explains: "It is not for you to know times or seasons" (Acts 1:7 NKJV).

Christ didn't challenge or correct their kingdom conception. Why? Could it be the apostles were correct? That Jesus will establish a kingdom on earth? Scripture is not shy about this promise. Examine the itinerary of your journey home, and you will find ten centuries reserved by God for him to do what he promised to do—establish Eden. Place your ear upon the pages of your Bible and you will hear the hoofbeats of a coming king.

I do.

As I've discussed and taught this topic, I've detected varying levels of interest. Some are fascinated by this discussion. They relish any message about the millennium.

Others? They may or may not say it out loud, but they are thinking, *What*

Examine the itinerary of your journey home, and you will find ten centuries reserved by God for him to do what he promised to do—establish Eden. Place your ear upon the pages of your Bible and you will hear the hoofbeats of a coming king.

does this matter? It all works out in the end. They are "pan-millennialists." It all pans out, and that's all they need to know.

I get it. That's okay.

Whether you like no details or abundant details, what matters is this: a glorious day awaits God's children. It seems to include an interlude of earthly abundance. It most certainly includes an eternity of joy in God's presence. Your longings for a world made right will become a reality. Our Father has a plan, and he holds us in his hand.

When my daughters were toddlers, we had a sophisticated bedtime routine. The girls knew how to extend our goodnight time so they wouldn't have to go to sleep. "Be funny, Daddy," they'd say. And I would comply. I'd bump my nose on the door or trip and fall on the floor. They'd laugh and then say, "Be goofy, Daddy." I'd comply with a clown face and silly expressions. They'd laugh again, but they wouldn't let me leave without responding to one final request. "Be strong, Daddy."

I'd flex my muscles. I'd stand tall like a grizzly and chase all the shadows away.

I like to think that the sight of a strong daddy helped them settle down and sleep.

It certainly helps us, right?

We have a strong Father. Strong enough to make a million galaxies, yet near enough to chase away every shadow of the night.

Keep looking to him. Keep singing "Joy to the World."

Joy to the world! The Lord is come.
Let earth receive her King
Let every heart prepare Him room
And Heaven and nature sing
And Heaven and nature sing
And Heaven, and Heaven, and nature sing.

PART 2

What's Next and Why It Matters

I PASSED TWO FULL DECADES on this earth before I ever boarded a subway train. In my West Texas hometown, we never considered underground travel. We drilled underground for oil, hunted underground for snakes, pumped underground for water, but travel underground in a train? Never an option.

You can understand my consternation, then, the first time I found myself riding on a subway train beneath the metropolis of São Paulo, Brazil. Four college buddies and I were spending the summer in the city. Our assignment was to be of service to the missionaries. I don't know what we hoped to accomplish. We didn't speak the language. None of us had ever lived overseas. We'd never played football with a round ball. We were the greenest of gringos. Still, we were there to be of help. When one of the missionaries told a couple of us to take the subway across the city to run an errand, I don't recall confessing our inexperience.

The two of us located the subway station and figured out how to board the train. But as it raced through the dark, we realized we didn't know where we were going, nor did we know when or how to get off. We stood in the aisle, gripping leather ceiling straps and asking each other questions.

"What do we do next?"

"How do we know where we exit?"

"How do you say 'help!' in Portuguese?"

We surveyed the crowd of passengers. People read newspapers, thumbed through novels. Some of them even dozed off. How could they be so tranquil? We were riding a bullet through a tunnel! What did they know that we didn't?

A gracious, English-speaking Brazilian overheard our banter and came to our rescue.

"Americanos?"

We nodded.

"Lost?"

We nodded again.

"Need help?"

We handed him the note of paper that bore the name of our destination. He pointed to a linear map stretched over the windows inside the car.

"That is a map of this subway route." He pointed to a dot on the line. "We are nearing that station." He then pointed to a dot some six or seven names down the line. "That is your destination. As we pass through each stop, take note. You'll be getting closer and closer. Once you see the name of your station, get off."

He made it sound easy. And it was! We exited at the right station. Everything changed once we knew there was a map.

Did you know God has provided a map for us? My best attempt at the sequence for what happens next looks like this:

HEAVEN'S TIME LINE

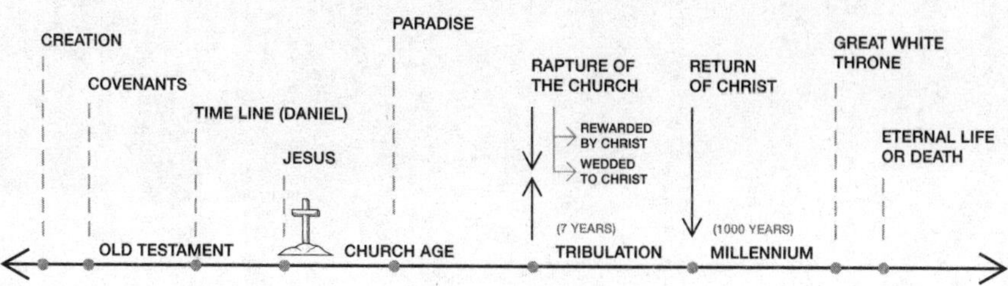

No person can claim to have an airtight forecast of the future. Only God knows the details of tomorrow. However, we can claim this promise: "[The Holy Spirit] will tell you what is yet to come" (John 16:13). God spent a great deal of time and ink telling us what to expect. It honors him and does the soul good to ponder his plans.

In the book of Revelation, God is identified as "Almighty" eight different times.[1] The Greek term is *pantokrator*—a compound of two Greek words: *panto* (everything) and *kratein* (to hold). God holds everything! At the helm of history is a God who not only rules the age but controls the calendar. We can speculate about the order of events, but we need never wonder about the certainty of the outcome. He holds the world in his hands.

Most people ride through life like novice gringos on a subway train, clueless as to where they are going and how they will get off. On the São Paulo subway, my friend and I were two anxious passengers surrounded by a carful of calm ones. In our society the ratio is inverted; confusion is rampant, and tranquility is rare.

Want to know the secret of peaceful passage?

Know where the subway train of history is headed.

CHAPTER 6

The People of Paradise

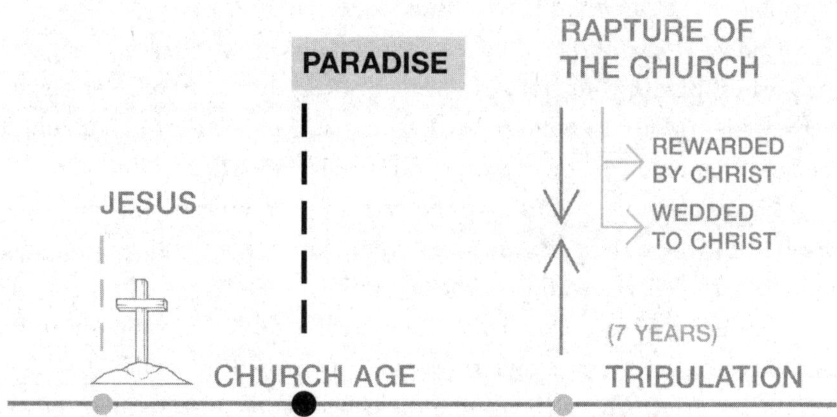

TED WILLIAMS, THE GREATEST HITTER in the history of major league baseball, hangs out in a one-story warehouse near the Scottsdale, Arizona, airport. He's been there since the day after his death in 2002.

His curators don't like the word *death*. The Alcor Life Extension Program prefers to say he "ended his first life cycle." While they neither confirm nor deny the slugger's presence in their facility, his daughter does.

When he died—excuse me, when he "ended his first life cycle" at the age of eighty-three—he was packed in a crate of ice, flown to Arizona, injected with a form of human deicer, and placed in a stainless-steel bay where he and fifty-eight other residents await their Lazarus moment at -196 degrees C. They banked their bodies in the hope of reanimation—that someone someday will poke a needle or push a button and trigger life cycle number two.[1]

One can hardly fault the MVP for wanting another trip to the plate. No one, especially the batting champ, wants to hear the words "You're out." Most people dread that moment. They are held in "slavery by their fear of death" (Heb. 2:15).

Epicurus, who died in 270 BC, described death as the "most dreaded of evils."[2] The seventeenth-century philosopher Thomas Hobbes deemed his death as "my last voyage, a great leap in the dark."[3] Robert Green Ingersoll, one of America's most outspoken agnostics, could offer no words of hope at his brother's funeral. "Life is a narrow vale between the cold and barren peaks of two eternities. We strive in vain to look beyond the heights."[4]

Such sad, depressing language! Can't we aspire for something greater than "a great leap in the dark"? Frame death in a more positive light than "dreaded evil"? Our good God tells us we can.

"End of story?" he challenges. "Quite the contrary! Death triggers the greatest part of your story." In heaven's diagram this sojourn is but the beginning—the first letter of the first sentence in the first paragraph of the first chapter of the great story God is writing with your life.

He sees our time on this earth not as the final performance, but as the casting call where the parts are announced. Life is not the beginning and ending, but solely the ending of the beginning.

Consider this assurance from the apostle Paul: "We want you to be quite certain, brothers, about those who have died, to make sure that you do not grieve about them, like the other people who have no hope" (1 Thess. 4:13 TJB).

The Thessalonian church had buried her share of loved ones, and Paul wanted the members who remained to be "quite certain" that their death was no reason for despair. Could you benefit from the same confidence?

- If you've buried a parent, you could.
- If cancer has taken the love of your life, you could.

In heaven's diagram this sojourn is but the beginning—the first letter of the first sentence in the first paragraph of the first chapter of the great story God is writing with your life.

- If your warm tears have fallen on the cold face of a friend, you could.
- If your child made it to heaven before making it to kindergarten, God speaks to you.

He transforms our hopeless grief into hope-filled grief. How? By telling us what happens when we die. If a Christian perishes before the rapture, that person's spirit immediately enters the presence of God, and that person enjoys conscious fellowship with the Father and with those who have gone before.

Where do we find such hope? In the answers to three vital questions.

Where Do We Go When We Die?

Paradise: the next stop on our journey. That is the term Jesus used with the dying thief on the cross. The crucified crook asked, "Remember me when you come into your kingdom" (Luke 23:42 NCV). Jesus, in a great act of grace, told him, "I tell you the truth, today you will be with me in paradise" (v. 43 NCV).

Is Paradise the same as heaven? Sort of.

John Wesley called Paradise "only the porch of Heaven."[5] It is the first stage of eternal rest; hors d'oeuvres of our heavenly feast. Paradise is not the final version of heaven, nor the ultimate expression of home. It is simply the gathering place of the saved until Christ comes for his children.

The Greek word for *paradise* refers to a walled park or garden. The word traces its origin to the Persian word *pairidaeza,* which designates an enclosed garden or royal park. Randy Alcorn explains: "Paradise was not generally understood as mere allegory . . . but as an actual physical place where God and his people lived together, surrounded by physical beauty, enjoying great pleasures and happiness."[6]

That means early readers of Jesus' promise to the thief would have seen the word *paradise* and thought of Eden's garden. The term conjured up images of a tangible, touchable location. Adam and Eve didn't walk amid stardust or cloudy vapors. Their feet felt the firm earth, nostrils inhaled perfumed air, skin felt the warm sun, lips tasted sweetened fruit. Paradise was a real garden with physical features.

Why would we think heaven's Paradise is any different? In Jesus' second reference to Paradise, he said: "To him who overcomes I will give to eat from the tree of life, which is in the midst of the Paradise of God" (Rev. 2:7 NKJV).

Note the tense of the sentence. The tree *is* in the midst of Paradise. Could this be the original tree? There is no indication it was ever destroyed. "After sending them out, the LORD God stationed mighty cherubim to the east of the Garden of Eden. And he placed a flaming sword that flashed back and forth to guard the way to the tree of life" (Gen. 3:24 NLT).

Angels protect God's garden. It has a special place in the plan and heart of God. Could it not occupy the center of Paradise? If so, your loved ones see the garden of Eden. Whatever can be said of the garden can be said of Paradise.

Where is Paradise? The Bible refers to three kinds of heaven. There is an atmospheric heaven. This is the sky or troposphere. It includes the breathable atmosphere that blankets the earth (Gen. 7:11–12). There is a planetary heaven. This layer encompasses our mighty and majestic universe.

And then there is the third heaven. Paradise. It exists outside our physical universe. Paul was privileged to have a peek into this realm:

> I was caught up to the third heaven fourteen years ago. Whether I was in my body or out of my body, I don't know—only God knows. Yes, only God knows whether I was in my body or outside my body. But I do know that I was caught up to paradise and heard things so astounding that they cannot be expressed in words, things no human is allowed to tell. (2 Cor. 12:2–4 NLT)

Paul was "caught up to the third heaven." The experience was so splendid that he didn't know if he was in or out of his body! He heard things too astounding for words. What he experienced was so otherworldly that he was prohibited to share the details!

To think, this is what our deceased loved ones are experiencing. An unspeakably splendid realm.

It is not the domain of the dead but the land of superabundant life. It is not a foggy valley of spooky spirits but a joyful community of saints. Jesus insisted that Abraham, Isaac, and Jacob are not dead but living (Matt. 22:32). Paul referred to the citizenry of Paradise as "saints in light" (Col. 1:12 ESV).

Paradise is almost heaven but not quite. It is grand but temporary lodging. The eternal form of heaven will begin after the millennium. God has a cosmic remodeling on his time line: a universe forever purged of sin and populated by lovers of God. As Peter wrote, "We are looking forward to a new heaven and a new earth, where righteousness dwells" (2 Peter 3:13).

> Paradise is almost heaven but not quite. It is grand but temporary lodging.

Until then, this much is clear: dead believers are not dead. They enjoy the presence of God. And as nothing unholy can dwell in God's presence, we can be sure they have been made holy as well.

When Do We Leave for Paradise?

Immediately upon death. This was the promise Jesus gave the thief on the cross: "I tell you the truth, *today* you will be with me in paradise" (Luke 23:43 NCV, emphasis mine).

I have a hunch the thief was hoping to be remembered in some far-off future event when the kingdom comes. Boy, was he in for a surprise. He went from torture to triumph in the blink of an eye. The spirit of the thief was instantaneously swept into the presence of God. We can expect the same. The spirit of the believer journeys home while the body of the believer awaits the resurrection.

Perhaps you've heard the phrase "to be absent from the body is to be at home with the Lord." Paul coined it: "We . . . would prefer to be away from the body and at home with the Lord" (2 Cor. 5:8).

At the rapture our bodies will be resurrected. But Paul was not speaking of the rapture in this verse. Otherwise, he would not have used the phrase "away from the body." Paul was describing a phase after our death and before the resurrection of our bodies. During this time we will be "at home with the Lord."

Elsewhere Paul wrote: "For to me, to live is Christ and to die is gain. If I am to go on living in the body, this will mean fruitful labor for me. Yet what shall I choose? I do not know! I am torn between the two: I desire to depart and be with Christ, which is better by far" (Phil. 1:21–23).

The grammar used here suggests an immediate departure of the spirit after death.[7]

As Stephen was being martyred, he saw "heaven open and the Son of Man standing at God's right side" (Acts 7:56 NCV). As he was near death, he prayed, "Lord Jesus, receive my spirit" (v. 59 NCV). It is safe to assume that Jesus did exactly that. Though the body of Stephen was dead, his spirit was alive. Though his body was buried, his spirit was in the presence of Jesus himself.

Some suggest otherwise. Teachers have proposed a transitional period of penance, a "holding tank" in which we are punished for our sins. This "purgatory" is the place where, for an undetermined length of time, we receive what our sins deserve so that we can rightly receive what God has prepared.

Two problems derail this idea. First, none of us can endure what our sins deserve. Second, Jesus already has. The wages of sin is death, not purgatory (Rom. 6:23). The Bible also teaches that Jesus became our purgatory and took our punishment: ". . . upholding all things by the word of his power, making purgation of sins . . . " (Heb. 1:3 DRA). Our purgatory occurred at Calvary when Jesus endured it for our sake.

Others feel that while the body is buried, the spirit is asleep. They come by their conviction honestly enough. Seven different times in two different epistles, Paul used the term *sleep* to refer to death (1 Cor. 11:30; 15:6, 18, 20; 1 Thess. 4:13–15). One could certainly deduce that the time between death and the return of Christ is spent sleeping. (And, if such is the case, who would complain? We could certainly use the rest.)

But there is one problem. When the Bible refers to those who have already died, they are anything but slumbering. Their bodies are inactive, but their spirits are wide awake. Matthew 17:3 speaks of Moses and Elijah, who appeared on the Mount of Transfiguration with Jesus. Christ depicted Lazarus and the rich man as conscious in Paradise and Hades after they died (Luke 16:22–31). Scripture speaks of "thousands upon thousands of angels in joyful assembly" being joined by "the spirits of the righteous made perfect" (Heb. 12:22–23). And what about the cloud of witnesses who surround us (Heb. 12:1)? Couldn't these be the heroes of our faith and the loved ones who have gone before?

There is no lapse, no time-out, no reformatory or probation. The moment believers take their final breath on earth, they have their first glimpse of heaven. Which raises another question.

What Will We Do in Paradise?

The first order of business will be the healing of the soul. In Jesus' story of the rich man and Lazarus, the latter was a beggar. He was "full of sores" and was laid at the rich man's gate (Luke 16:20 NKJV). Can a more pitiful sight be conjured? His body was covered in ulcerated, open wounds.

Each day he was loaded in a cart, carried to the property of the mansion, placed on the ground, and left there. When the rich man's servants threw scraps on the street, Lazarus hoped to snatch what he could from the leftovers—a crust of bread, a chunk of meat.

He was a homeless beggar. In our world he would have slept on the street or under an overpass. How many times did he overhear the barbs of passersby? "Go to work!" "The guy needs to get a job." "What a waste of life."

The sores on his flesh were horrendous, but the sores on his spirit? Rejection upon rejection. Left to scrape by in the shadow of a rich man's house. Daily reminded of how little he mattered in society.

But then, in a moment, the destinies were reversed. Both men died, and Lazarus was "carried by the angels to Abraham's bosom" (16:22 NKJV). Radiant ambassadors of heaven winged Lazarus into the presence of Abraham, the most famous of the Hebrew heroes. The contrast could not be more dramatic. The father of Israel and a lowly pauper. There in view of all of Paradise, Lazarus was comforted, honored, blessed, and healed.

Each of us lives with inner wounds, bruises, and lacerations, the result of life in a harsh world. If our unseen selves were made visible, we would resemble tortured POWs. How many of us have the outward appearance of health but on the inside bear the lacerations left by harsh tongues, overbearing parents, or rejection?

Yet, all wounds will be healed in Paradise.

Once healed, we will ponder the glory of God.

According to a story, a man had one day to explore Yosemite National Park. He stopped at the ranger station and explained his situation. "If you only had one day to explore Yosemite, what would you do?"

The ranger looked at the tourist and said, "Sir, if I had only one day in Yosemite, I'd sit by the Merced River and cry."[8]

Gratefully, we will have no limitations on our exploration of our Maker and his universe.

"Oh, the depth of the riches and wisdom and knowledge of God! How unsearchable are his judgments and how inscrutable his ways!" (Rom. 11:33 ESV). Don't assume we will ever exhaust our study of God. Endless attributes await us. His grace will increasingly stun, wisdom progressively astound, and perfection ever more sharpen into focus. Our minds will be healthy, imaginations pure. No more lust, regrets, or guilt. No more wasted thoughts. Our attention span will match our opportunity to use it!

Since we are made in the image of our Creator, we will create. We sometimes dread heaven because we fear boredom. Earth seems more interesting because earth has activity. Who would think God would have creative work for us in Paradise? Then again, who would have thought God would give work to Adam? But he did. God paraded birds and beasts past Adam like a Thanksgiving Day spectacular. And Adam put his brand-new brain to work.

Can't we expect to do the same? What do you suppose your departed loved ones are creating? Can you see her humming a new melody? Envision him designing an archway? Creating the ultimate game of chess, a breathtaking watercolor, or an astonishing poem?

Paradise is not populated by clueless clones or lobotomized spirits, but by curious, happy, and . . . prayerful saints. Really? Do saints in heaven pray for the saints on earth? I believe the answer is yes, for this reason: Jesus prays (Rom. 8:34), and we will be like him. Christ, at this moment, intercedes for us. "When Christ appears, we shall be like him, for we shall see him as he is" (1 John 3:2).

People of Paradise comprise the church triumphant and the church militant. Triumphant in the sense of eternal victory, militant in the sense of persistent intercession. They pray that God's justice be done and his children preserved.

But how do they do this without a body? Paradise is that time in which the Christian is "absent from the body and . . . present with the Lord" (2 Cor. 5:8 NKJV). So if the body is in the grave and the spirit is in Paradise, how does the spirit behave like a body?

Paul offered a clue: "Meanwhile we groan, longing to be clothed instead with our heavenly dwelling" (2 Cor. 5:2). Paul may have been referring to the abode of heaven. Or he may have been referring to a body given to us for our time in Paradise. Not flesh and blood, since flesh and blood cannot inherit the kingdom (1 Cor. 15:50), but perhaps some form of ethereal vehicle as we await our glorified bodies?

Paradise is not populated by clueless clones or lobotomized spirits, but by curious, happy, and . . . prayerful saints.

Consider the appearance of Moses and Elijah. They came to Jesus on the Mount of Transfiguration and "what a glorious appearance they made! They talked over his exodus, the one Jesus was about to complete in Jerusalem" (Luke 9:30–31 MSG). Moses had been dead for twelve hundred years and Elijah eight hundred. Yet they were still distinct, recognizable, and able to communicate with Christ about things to come.

The people of Paradise enjoy a much better but still incomplete state. They anticipate the new heaven and earth, the glorified body to be received at the rapture, and—this may surprise you—they look forward to the arrival of the rest of the saints.

We can thank the author of the book of Hebrews for this point. In chapter 11 he highlights the lives of Sarah, Isaac, Jacob, Moses, and Rahab the harlot. If he had more time (his words, not mine), he would have shared the stories of Gideon, Barak, Samson, Jephthah, David, Samuel, and the prophets. "All these people earned a good reputation because of their faith, yet none of them received all that God had promised" (Heb. 11:39 NLT).

We expect the next verse to tell us, "They have received it all now." But the writer surprises, even stuns, us by describing how the saints are waiting for the rest of us. "God had a better plan for us: that their faith and our faith would come together to make one completed whole, their lives of faith not complete apart from ours" (Heb. 11:40 MSG).

That last sentence deserves a double reading. *Their lives are not complete without ours.* The saints are waiting on us to show up!

If you've ever been a part of a family holiday celebration, you know exactly what this means. I'm the youngest of four children. By the time I was old enough to enjoy Christmas, my two older sisters had husbands and homes of their own. The big moment of Christmas was less the coming of Santa and more the coming of my siblings. The sound of the car in the driveway and the voices in the doorway were great signals. We're all back together again!

As long as one family member is gone, something is missing. As wonderful as Paradise is, it won't be complete until all God's children are home.

The big party won't start until the last one of us crosses the river.

The early church fathers embraced this truth. Cyprian (AD 200–258) wrote a letter to his friend Cornelius, the bishop of Rome. Both were expecting martyrdom. The first appealed to the second: "If one of us goes before the other, let our love for one another be unbroken, when we are with the Lord; let our prayers for our brethren and sisters be unceasing."[9]

Charles Wesley expressed his affection for the entirety of the church in his hymn "Come, Let Us Join Our Friends Above":

One family we dwell in him,
One Church, above, beneath,
Though now divided by the stream,
The narrow stream of death:
Ev'n now by faith we join our hands
With those that went before,
And greet the blood-besprinkled bands
On the eternal shore.[10]

Saints in heaven can encourage saints on earth. We are never instructed to pray to them or invoke their presence, but we can be sure they pray for us and invoke God's power in our lives.

Early in the next chapter, the author of Hebrews urged, "Therefore, since we are surrounded by such a huge crowd of witnesses to the life of faith, let us strip off every weight that slows us down, especially the sin that so easily trips us up. And let us run with endurance the race God has set before us" (Heb. 12:1 NLT).

The writer envisioned a great stadium of spiritual athletes. The stands are filled with the Abrahams, Josephs, and Marthas from all generations and nations. They have completed their own events and now witness the races of their spiritual, if not physical, descendants.

They are alive! They aren't pictures in a gallery or names in a book but God-lovers in a crowded stadium cheering for those who run on the track.

I find such encouragement in this. Hanging in the room adjacent to our church platform is a Ron DiCianni painting entitled *The Cloud of Witnesses.* It portrays an earnest preacher holding an open Bible encircled by half a dozen evangelists from earlier generations. Elijah and his scrolls. Paul and his pen. They stand behind the young preacher as he preaches, urging him on. As I step toward my pulpit, I like to imagine them calling my name: "Give 'em heaven, Max!"

Who stands behind you? Health professionals: Do caregivers from centuries past applaud you? Schoolteachers: Might you sense the encouragement of tutors, professors, and instructors who have preceded you? Farmers, carpenters, soldiers: Does the cloud of witnesses include your coworkers from another continent and era?

At this moment, in every moment, you are watched by millions of loving eyes. "Since we are surrounded . . . let us run with endurance the race God has set before us" (Heb. 12:1 NLT).

Listen carefully, the passage compels, and you will hear a vast multitude of God's family. Noah is among them. So is Mary the mother of Jesus. Your elementary school teacher shouts your name. So does an uncle you never knew. Do you hear the support of the first-century believers? What about the Chinese house church martyrs or the eighteenth-century missionaries to Africa? Some of us have mom and dad, brother or sister—even a child in the stands. They are part of the people of Paradise.

If, perchance, this book outlives the life of its author, then be assured, dear reader, I will be exhorting you from Paradise. If these pages are read by my descendants, grandchildren and great-grandchildren, I urge you to

At this moment, in every moment, you are watched by millions of loving eyes. "Since we are surrounded . . . let us run with endurance the race God has set before us" (Heb. 12:1 NLT).

incline an ear toward the skies. I'm shouting your name! Applauding your faith! Celebrating your lives!

Be assured that Epicurus missed the mark. Death is not the most dreaded of evils. Thomas Hobbes was wrong. Death is not a leap in the dark. Ted Williams was a great baseball player, but his death preparation didn't even get him to first base. Human deep freeze won't defeat death.

But God can and God has. And because God has, we can die with faith. After all, what is the downside of death? For the believer, there is none. Ask yourself, "What's the worst thing that death can do to me?" Then read and reread Romans 8:35, 38–39. "Who shall separate us from the love of Christ? . . . Neither death nor life, neither angels nor demons, neither the present nor the future, nor any powers, neither height nor depth, nor anything else in all creation, will be able to separate us from the love of God that is in Christ Jesus our Lord."

My friend Calvin Miller wrote:

> I once scorned ev'ry fearful thought of death,
> When it was but the end of pulse and breath,
> But now my eyes have seen past that pain
> There's a world that's waiting to be claimed.
> Earthmaker, Holy, let me now depart,
> For living's such a temporary art.
> And dying is but getting dressed for God,
> Our graves are merely doorways of sod.[11]

Linvel Baker would echo that thought. He preached for forty years in the small towns of Texas. Everyone who knew him loved him. His final years brought some health challenges. A couple of minor cardiac events. A heart valve replacement. A serious bout with COVID. He chose to retire at the age of sixty-five.

He spent his final earthly day on his recently acquired 150 undeveloped ranchland acres. He and his brother, Lauris, did what they had done so often in their youth. They pitched rocks, shot at watermelons, talked about life. As the sun set, Lauris headed home, leaving Linvel alone.

No one knows for sure what happened next, but piecing together details of the doctor's report and the police assessment, it went something like this.

Linvel had a heart attack. He knew the symptoms. He also knew there wasn't time for first responders to reach him. He set down his cell phone and, no doubt clutching his chest, stumbled to the top of the rise where he and his wife, Shirley, had planned to build their retirement home. He sat down near a grove of oak trees and removed his boots. He lay back on the ground with arms outstretched and face toward heaven—and died.

His son-in-law found him with "peace written all over his face."[12]

Those who knew Linvel well were not surprised at his final acts. Like Moses at the burning bush, Linvel understood he was about to step onto holy ground. So he removed his boots and entered Paradise. That's how a good man dies.

Wouldn't you love to do likewise?

CHAPTER 7

The Rebel and the Rescue

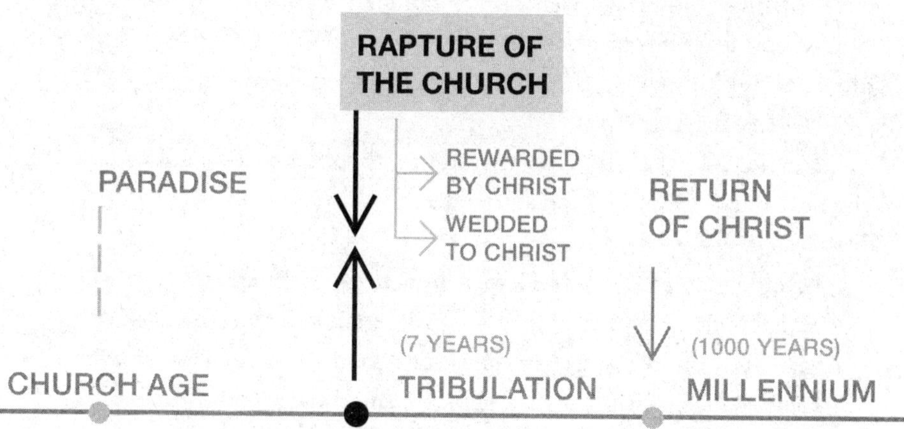

THE DATE 9/11 STIRS a hornet's nest of memories. Those of us who are old enough to recall the attacks of that day can do so vividly. Two planes crashing into two towers in New York, another plane ablaze in a Pennsylvania field. The Pentagon burning. Ash-covered New Yorkers running. Heroic firefighters rushing.

Flights were grounded. Work came to a standstill. The military was placed on high alert. The world, it seemed, descended into a state of chaos.

I was in my church office that Tuesday. I'd barely taken a seat at my desk when Karen, my assistant, threw open the door and announced, "You need to see what is happening!" We hurried down the hall to a television. We watched in silence as the first tower tumbled, then the second.

No one knew what to think. *Are we at war? Are other planes about to crash into other cities?* We had no clue.

Yet, for all I didn't know, there was one thing of which I was dead certain. So I got busy.

I phoned Denalyn and told her my plan. She agreed. She jumped into her car. I climbed into mine. We each drove to the nearby schools where our daughters were students.

I didn't bother with a permission request. I bypassed the administration office and walked straight to the sixth-grade classroom. The teacher saw me standing in the doorway and deduced the reason for my presence.

"Sara," she instructed, "go with your father." Sara grabbed her backpack and complied. Meanwhile, at a different building, Denalyn was doing the same with our two older daughters.

Within minutes we were all at home. I wanted us to be together. Something fearful was afoot, and there was no way our kids would face it alone. So we kidnapped them. We snatched them away.

We *harpazoed* them.

Harpazo. That is the Greek word used by the apostle Paul to describe the next major event on God's calendar.

> According to the Lord's word, we tell you that we who are still alive, who are left until the coming of the Lord, will certainly not precede those who have fallen asleep. For the Lord himself will come down from heaven, with a loud command, with the voice of the archangel and with the trumpet call of God, and the dead in Christ will rise first. After that, we who are still alive and are left will be caught up [*harpazoed*] together with them in the clouds to meet the Lord in the air. And so we will be with the Lord forever. Therefore encourage one another with these words. (1 Thess. 4:15–18)

The verb *harpazo* translates into the English *seize*, *snatch* (in Latin *rapere*, from which comes the English word *rapture*). The word describes a most mysterious miracle, a moment in which living believers will be instantly changed into their resurrection bodies and lifted into heaven to meet Jesus. The bodies of dead believers will be resurrected and reunited with their spirits. The mortal will take on immortality. Both groups will be "caught up"[1] to meet Christ in the air and will be taken into Paradise.

A breathtaking thought, don't you agree? A generation of Christians will skip the cemetery. Modern-day Elijahs and Enochs they will be. Elijah was caught up in a chariot (2 Kings 2:11). Enoch never died (Heb. 11:5). No final breath or death. Just one moment here, the next moment there.

What I did for my daughters, God will do for his children. He will come for his family. But why? What purpose does the rapture serve? How can I believe it will take place?

The prophecy we reviewed in chapter 4 provides part of the answer. The angel Gabriel told Daniel: "That leader will make firm an agreement with many people for seven years. He will stop the offerings and sacrifices after three and one-half years. A destroyer will do blasphemous things until the ordered end comes to the destroyed city" (Dan. 9:27 NCV).

You just read one of the Bible's earliest references to a time of severe tribulation: seven years in which the entire world will feel the oppression of an evil ruler. Gabriel called him "the destroyer." He makes it clear that:

A Bad Dude Is A-Comin'

Antichrist is the name most used for this scoundrel. He is, quite literally, *anti*-Christ. He is anti-salvation, anti-hope, anti-forgiveness, and anti-truth. *Anti* can also mean "instead of." This evil leader will want people to worship him instead of Jesus.

More than one hundred passages of Scripture allude to him.[2] They describe the origin, character, career, conquest, and doom of this final world ruler. Clearly, God wants his people to know something about this prince of darkness. Gabriel described him to Daniel with these words:

> When rebels have become completely wicked, a fierce-looking king, a master of intrigue, will arise. He will become very strong, but not by his own power. He will cause astounding devastation and will succeed in whatever he does. He will destroy those who are mighty, the holy people. He will

> cause deceit to prosper, and he will consider himself superior. When they feel secure, he will destroy many and take his stand against the Prince of princes. Yet he will be destroyed, but not by human power. (Dan. 8:23–25)

This paragraph reads like a table of contents in the biography of the Antichrist.

He will come "when rebels have become completely wicked." Something will trigger a tsunami of evil. During a time of immorality, depravity, barbarism, and terrorism, he will appear on the world stage. The term for this era of anarchy is the tribulation. Are we in that stage of evil? Not yet. But it seems to be nearing.

The Antichrist will be a "fierce-looking king, a master of intrigue." He will have an intimidating air about him. Ominous and pompous; filled with the fullness of Satan. Rakish. Genius. Charming. Perhaps his eyes will be beady and dark or his jaw strong and defiant. He will be the *master of intrigue*. That is to say he will be perceptive and cunning. It may mean he traffics in the world of the occult.[3]

In the book of Revelation, John says the Antichrist will have the mouth of a lion (13:2), which means he will command attention with his voice. He will mesmerize the world with his arrogant words. He will be a soul-captivating orator, hypnotic in his shrewdness and language. He will even claim to be God.

"He will become very strong, but not by his own power." The Antichrist is the devil's proxy. Just as Satan entered Judas on the day of betrayal, so Satan will enter this person (John 13:27 and Rev. 13:2).

He will rise from obscurity as a great peacemaker. "That leader will make firm an agreement with many people for seven years" (Dan. 9:27 NCV). The olive branch will be his gift. He will negotiate a seven-year treaty with the nation of Israel and be celebrated as a great diplomat. Yet, midway through the treaty, he will break it—and all hell will break loose.

"He will cause astounding devastation and succeed in whatever he does." Chapters 6 through 19 of Revelation describe in detail what will happen during the oppression by the Antichrist. Those scriptures refer to famine, death, and cosmic disturbances. J. Dwight Pentecost wrote these sobering words: "No passage can be found to alleviate to any degree whatsoever the severity of this time that shall come upon the earth."[4]

"He will destroy those who are mighty, the holy people." People who find faith during the tribulation will be attacked. In addition, the Jewish remnant will feel the full force of his anti-Semitic ire.

The Antichrist will cause "deceit to prosper." Under his leadership, deception and dishonesty will be standard fare.

"When they feel secure, he will destroy many and take his stand against the Prince of princes. Yet he will be destroyed, but not by human power." The great news: the Antichrist will be destroyed in the end. The bad news: the world must see him first.

Combine the putrid spirits of Stalin, Hitler, Pol Pot, Mao Tse-tung, and Idi Amin with every other arrogant ruler in history and you have a glimpse of the Antichrist on his nice days. No wonder Jesus warned the tribulation generation: "When you see Jerusalem being surrounded by armies, you will know that its desolation is near. Then let those who are in Judea flee to the mountains, let those in the city get out, and let those in the country not enter the city. For this is the time of punishment in fulfillment of all that has been written" (Luke 21:20–22).

I know what you are thinking: *Max, I am so inspired. Thank you for this wonderful chapter! All this talk about the Antichrist, evil, total destruction—why, I am ready to face my day.*

I know. Depressing. I'm describing the darkest chapter of human history. But I'm not finished. I've not yet told you the good news. And my, oh my, do I have good news to share!

The tribulation? It's going to happen. Satan's henchman? He will be worse than anyone can imagine. But the wonderful news? If you are in Christ, you won't have to face him. For by the time he arrives, you will be long gone. A bad dude is a-comin', but before he does . . .

All Believers Will Be Leaving

In the same way that Denalyn and I protected our kids from impending trouble, Jesus will *harpazo* us.

> For the Lord himself will come down from heaven, with a loud command, with the voice of the archangel and with the trumpet call of God,

> and the dead in Christ will rise first. After that, we who are still alive and are left will be caught up together with them in the clouds to meet the Lord in the air. And so we will be with the Lord forever. Therefore encourage one another with these words. (1 Thess. 4:16–18)

Christians, upon the signal of Christ, will be transported into the presence of Christ. This rescue could happen at any moment. It will be activated by the conclusion of the church age. Or, as Paul wrote, when "the full number of the Gentiles come in" (Rom. 11:25 RSV; see also Luke 21:24). God knows the name of every person who will be saved. In my imagination I see one of the angels standing next to the Book of Life, checking name after name until the "full number" of God's flock has come in. At that moment history's greatest evacuation event will occur.

The Lord will come with "a loud command." This is a classical Greek word (*keleusma*) used to describe a general when he addresses his army, an admiral when he speaks to his fleet, a charioteer when he drives his steeds.[5] Each issues their commands with authority. Christ will do likewise.

At his side will be the archangel. The sole figure identified in the Bible as an archangel is Michael. He is always depicted as the great foe of Satan. He is the one who declares, "Salvation, and strength, and the kingdom of our God, and the power of His Christ have come" (Rev. 12:10 NKJV). We will hear the voice of Michael at the rapture.

We will also hear a trumpet.

In the days of the Roman empire, soldiers learned to respond to three types of trumpets. The first prompted the troops to rise and strike their tents. The second trumpet announced it was time to fall into line. The third was the signal to march away. This is the last trumpet.

Christ will signal for us to march away—either out of the grave or off the earth—and "we will be with the Lord forever."

Envisioning the rapture reminds me of a job I had during Christmas break in college. I worked in a machine shop. One of my tasks was to sweep the floor at the end of the day. My dustpan would be littered with trash, dirt, wood shavings, and assorted junk. The pile also included a random collection of nails, nuts, bolts, and screws. The machinists might need these. Separating the good stuff from the bad stuff was easy. Just hover a magnet over the trash. Every item that contained the same properties of the magnet would rise out of the box and attach to it. Everything else was left behind.

The rapture will have a similar effect. Jesus will appear in the sky, and all who share his nature—who house his Spirit, who have within them the presence of Christ—will be caught up by his magnetic presence to meet him in the air.

Jesus said: "I tell you, on that night two people will be sleeping in one bed; one will be taken and the other will be left. There will be two women grinding grain together; one will be taken, and the other will be left" (Luke 17:34–35 NCV).

A modern translation of that passage would read: two people will be sipping coffee at a café; one will be taken and the other left. Two people will be watching a movie; one will be taken, the other left.

When we see Jesus, "he will change our humble bodies and make them like his glorified body" (Phil. 3:21 GW). Goodbye, cancer. Farewell, deformity. Hello healing, renewal, and restoration.

In 1684 Scottish Presbyterian Robert Baillie learned that he would be hanged for his faith, then drawn and quartered. In a nod to Philippians 3:21, Baillie replied: "They may hack and hew my body as they please, but I know assuredly nothing will be lost, but that all these my members shall be wonderfully gathered and made like Christ's glorious body."[6]

At the rapture the bodies of Christians will be raised and reconstituted to resemble the risen body of our Lord. When Jesus rose on Easter, he took on a body that was the prototype of the ones we'll have throughout eternity.

His glorified body was like his pre-crucifixion body. He could touch and be touched. He ate and drank. Yet, he also passed through walls and appeared in various locations without any visible means of transportation. Most significantly, he ascended into Paradise.

We will do the same.

The father of Matthew Robison was imagining such a miracle when he commissioned a grave marker for his son. The stone statue portrays the figure of a boy rising out of a wheelchair, arms extended toward the skies. Deprived of oxygen at birth, Matthew spent his short eleven years mostly blind and paralyzed. But he, and countless others like him, will ascend to meet Christ in a brand-new body.[7]

What a moment of miracles this will be! All prayers for healing will

Jesus will appear in the sky, and all who share his nature—who house his Spirit, who have within them the presence of Christ—will be caught up by his magnetic presence to meet him in the air.

be answered. The enigma of how to interpret the carte blanche promise of Jesus will be solved. "Whatever you ask of me, I will do it for you" (John 16:23–24, paraphrased). He means exactly that. This is no over-promise. We need not explain it away or water it down. We just need to wait. It's only a matter of time.

This calling forth includes all God's children who were conceived yet never took a breath outside the womb. Miscarriages took many. Abortions took many. Christ will lay claim to them all. Are they not his creations? Does he not have power over life and death? They will live in glorified bodies.

This raptured population includes children who never reached the age of accountability. They lacked the maturity to decide for or against Christ. They are safe in his care. So are people who lacked the mental capacity to comprehend the salvation invitation. They will receive brand-new brains.

This resurrection of the righteous will occur "in a moment, in the twinkling of an eye" (1 Cor. 15:52 NKJV). The Greek word used for *moment* is *atomos*, from which we get our word *atom*. To the degree the atom is small, this event is quick. It will happen "in the twinkling of an eye." How long is the twinkle of an eye? It is too quick to measure. That is how long Jesus needs to collect his church.

When will the rapture take place? Some Bible students place the rapture during the tribulation, others after the tribulation. It seems best to position it before the years of trouble. I say this for several reasons.

First, Jesus compared this moment to the rescues of Noah and Lot (Matt. 24:37–39, Luke 17:28–37). Noah felt no raindrops. Lot felt no brimstone. In the same manner, I believe Jesus will emancipate his church, and we will not feel the evil of the Antichrist.

Second, Paul urged us to "encourage one another" (1 Thess. 4:18). How can we be encouraged if we are going to face the Antichrist and the tribulation? If such were the case, Paul would have said, "Warn one another." But he didn't. The rapture of the church is a reason for comfort and assurance. Yes, a bad dude is coming, but, yes, the church will be leaving. Consequently, be encouraged.*

After the rapture what will happen to us? You are going to love the

---

* Please see Bonus Material from Max, p. 189, for more reasons to position the rapture before the tribulation.

answer to that question. After I retrieved my daughters on 9/11, they enjoyed a day away from school and some hot chocolate. Jesus promises a wedding and a feast and the greatest reward ceremony in history. But that is a topic for the next two chapters.

It occurs to me how odd this teaching might sound. What a zany, wacko forecast of the future. The sudden ascension of saints. The consequential collapse of society. The appearance of a Palpatine-like leader from hell. *Are you kidding me? A person would have to be insane to believe such a thought. That is the craziest thing I have ever heard.*

I understand what you are saying. It sounds fantastical. Yet, before you write off the rapture, remember—this is how our God works. Did he not flood the earth? Did he not level the walls of Jericho? Did he not turn the Red Sea into a red carpet so the Hebrews could escape bondage? Plagues fell on Egypt in the days of Moses. Fire fell on Mount Carmel in the days of Elijah.

God is the God of divine interruptions. Holy surprises. Who could have imagined God living on earth? But he came. Who could've imagined God hanging on a cross? But he died. Who could have imagined the empty tomb? But he rose from the dead. He intervenes in mighty and miraculous ways.

He has before.

He will again.

In the meantime keep an eye toward the sky. Live in such a way that Christ will find you faithfully looking for him. "So always be ready, because you don't know the day your Lord will come" (Matt. 24:42 NCV).

A tourist visited a beautiful mansion in Switzerland. He was stunned by the gardens, not a weed anywhere. Seeing the gardener, the tourist asked, "How long have you worked here?"

"Twenty years," came the answer.

"Does the owner live here?"

"No. In all these years, I've only seen him four times."

"He must be grateful. You tend the grounds as if you expect him to return tomorrow."

"Oh, no. I tend them as if I expect him to return today."[8]

Let's do likewise. For all we know, our Master will do just that.

CHAPTER 8

Crowned by Christ

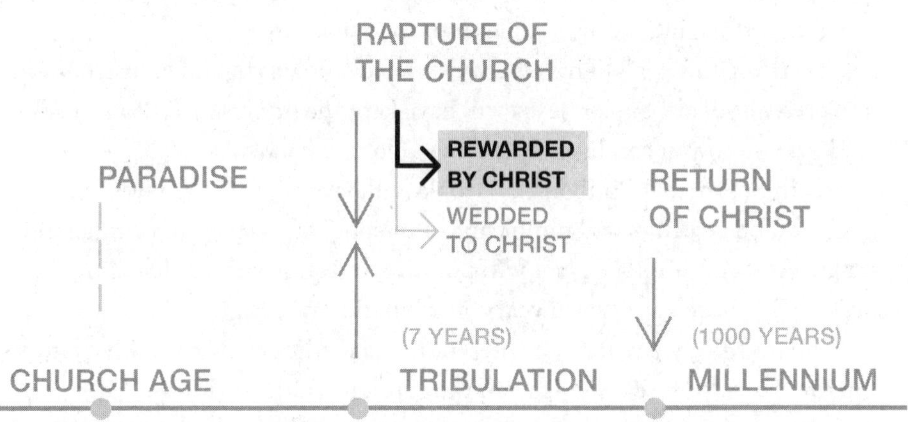

MILLIONS OF PEOPLE WATCHED the coronation of King Charles on May 6, 2023. The sovereign was crowned alongside Camilla, Queen Consort, at Westminster Abbey. Festivities stretched over three days. Pubs and bars remained open for an additional two hours each day. England observed Coronation Day as a national holiday. There were street parties and concerts.

Britain shelled out an estimated $125 million for the event.

Charles was anointed on hands, chest, and head with chrism oil made in Jerusalem using olives from the Mount of Olives. During the anointing he wore a pure white garment and the "Supertunica," a full-length gold silk coat.

He was then crowned with St. Edward's Crown, a solid-gold headpiece that dates to 1661. It is adorned by more than four hundred gemstones, including rubies and sapphires. Gun salutes were fired from military bases across the United Kingdom, and the British public was invited to make a pledge of loyalty to the crown: "I swear I will pay true allegiance to your majesty, and your heirs and successors. So help me God."

Then came processions and royal salutes, three cheers, and a flyby display using more than sixty aircraft.[1]

One big hullabaloo.

But compared to the one God has planned for you? It was a Cub Scout ceremony.

There is a crowning in your future. Not in Westminster Abbey, but in Paradise. Not by the Archbishop of Canterbury, but by Jesus. Surprised? Reluctant? Uncomfortable at the thought of being crowned by Christ? Hold that thought, and let's explore some context.

By this point we will have been extracted from earth and escorted into the presence of our Savior. Jesus will have kept the promise: "I'll come back and get you so you can live where I live" (John 14:3 MSG).

Millions, perhaps billions, of people will have vanished. Graves will be vacant. God-rejectors will tumble into a cesspool of violence and pandemonium. At some point a despot will promise to restore peace. He will sign a treaty with Israel, and seven years of tribulation will begin.

Thankfully, we will not be present to see it. We can be eternally grateful for "Jesus, who rescues us from the coming wrath" (1 Thess. 1:10).

As the chaos begins below, the celebration will have begun above.

Jesus Will Honor You

The Bible speaks of a reward ceremony that will take place in Paradise immediately after the rapture of the church. This event is called the judgment seat of Christ.

> For we will all stand before God's judgment seat. (Rom. 14:10)

> So we make it our goal to please him, whether we are at home in the body or away from it. For we must all appear before the judgment seat of Christ, so that each of us may receive what is due us for the things done while in the body, whether good or bad. (2 Cor. 5:9–10)

The Greek word translated *judgment* is *bēma*. The *bēma* is not a trial to ascertain whether we are innocent or guilty, saved or lost. That judgment occurs during our lifetime on earth. "People who believe in God's Son are not judged guilty. Those who do not believe have already been judged guilty, because they have not believed in God's one and only Son" (John 3:18 NCV).

The *bēma* judgment is not about salvation. It is about recognition. Salvation is based on Jesus' work for us. Our recognition is based on our work for him. Our deeds do not contribute to our salvation. Not one iota. That's a gift. Our deeds do, however, inform our reward.

The apostle Paul drew on a familiar image for this teaching. In the Greek games, after each contest the players stood before the *bēma*, an elevated seat on which the judge or emperor sat. There the winner received the crown, or laurel, of reward. Those who failed to win the race were not punished or cast out. They simply received no commendation.

So it will be at the judgment seat of Christ. Believers will be equally saved but not equally rewarded. In fact, some Christians will receive no reward at all. Paul described the works of some as "wood, hay, stubble" (1 Cor. 3:12 KJV). When tested by fire, these works don't survive.

> There is going to come a time of testing at Christ's Judgment Day to see what kind of material each builder has used. Everyone's work will be put through the fire so that all can see whether or not it keeps its value, and what was really accomplished. Then every workman who has built on the foundation with the right materials, and whose work still stands, will get his pay. But if the house he has built burns up, he will have a great loss. He himself will be saved, but like a man escaping through a wall of flames. (1 Cor. 3:13–15 TLB)

Salvation is based on Jesus' work for us. Our recognition is based on our work for him. Our deeds do not contribute to our salvation. Not one iota. That's a gift. Our deeds do, however, inform our reward.

What did Paul mean? "He himself will be saved, but like a man escaping through a wall of flames"? You could say, "He shall be saved by the skin of his teeth."

Some years ago I was called to the hospital bedside of a dying man. He had a reputation as a real rogue. He hosted parties at his plush house that would have made a porn star blush. Women, booze, and gambling. The guy did it all.

When the doctor told him to get his house in order, the fellow called me. The man I saw lying in the bed was a shell of the man he once was. Illness had taken his swagger. The prospect of death had sobered his thinking. He wanted to become a Christian.

By the time our conversation ended, he had asked Jesus for forgiveness. By the time I had driven home, he was in the presence of Jesus.

He is, I'm confident, saved by God's grace.

Yet, this person might be one of those who stand at the *bēma* with nothing in their hands. They have no trophy of love to lay at their Master's feet.

God loans each of us time, talent, and treasure. How we use them determines our recognition. Let's make it our aim to receive the crowns.

Our American culture has little or nothing to do with crowns. We inaugurate our leaders; we don't crown them. (Though there is a sense in which we'd like to crown a few of them.)

But even though we are a crownless society, we understand enough to know this: a king or queen could give no greater honor than a crown. The diadem is more than a bejeweled hat. It is a high endorsement. If you are crowned, then the supreme power in the land has given you a place at his table, a room in her castle, even a throne at his side. To be crowned is to be honored, applauded, and, most significantly, to be blessed.

In fact, the Bible interchanges the word *crown* with *blessing*. The epistles speak of being crowned; Jesus speaks of being blessed. "When the master comes and finds the servant doing his work, the servant will be blessed" (Matt. 24:46 NCV).

The Hebrew word for *bless* is a wealthy one. It literally means "to bow the knee."[2] The word was used in showing reverence and awe to an individual. The word's English cousins are *honor*, *endorse*, and *esteem*. The act is far more than a pat on the back or a casual "attaboy" but rather a moment in which you are endorsed by the most significant leader in your life. This is exactly what God did with Abraham when he promised: "I will make you into a great nation, and I will bless you" (Gen. 12:2).

Luke concluded his gospel with these words: "Jesus led his followers as far as Bethany, and he raised his hands and blessed them. While he was blessing them, he was separated from them and carried into heaven" (Luke 24:50–51 NCV).

To be blessed is to be validated. Even today, in parts of Brazil a child won't leave the house without his parents' blessing. Walking out the door they will ask, "*Benção, Papai?*" or "Blessing, Father?" What are they requesting? They seek an endorsement from the most significant leader of their life—their father. They don't want to leave the house without their father's approval.

Who would? Within each one of us is the longing to please our father.

Perhaps you never knew your father's blessing. Maybe you've lived your life in a canyon of silence, never knowing how your father felt about you. If so, you, more than anyone, will treasure the moment in heaven when your heavenly Father blesses you.

And we know what he will give you. Crowns will be distributed at the judgment.

The New Testament makes reference to two types of crowns. One is worn by rulers. The other is granted to victors. This is the imagery employed by the New Testament writers. (Think ancient Greek Olympics.) In the first century, athletes were given a laurel of woven vines and withered wild celery. Paul rightly called this a "corruptible crown." We, on the other hand, will receive incorruptible crowns in Paradise (1 Cor. 9:25 KJV).

At the age of thirteen, I entered the discus event at a track meet. I came in seventh place. Given the size of our small school, there could not have been more than nine or ten participants. The top three received medals. The top seven made a list of winners. I was so proud to see my name on the list! Seventh place and I strutted about like a peacock.

Imagine how we will feel when the Maker of the universe places a crown on our head.

Scripture mentions five crowns. It's appropriate to test the fit of each.

The Crown of Self-Control

"Everyone who competes in the games goes into strict training. They do it to get a crown that will not last, but we do it to get a crown that will last forever" (1 Cor. 9:25).

Jesus will applaud your "strict training." Life comes with temptations. The Spirit of God helps you and me say no to the cravings of the flesh. Your battle with the bottle? Your struggle with lust? The malicious temptation to overeat, overspend, overindulge? Your Master knows your challenge and will reward your diligence.

The Crown of Influence

"You are our hope, our joy, and the crown we will take pride in when our Lord Jesus Christ comes" (1 Thess. 2:19 NCV).

You're praying for a neighbor. You send money to a mission field. You're doing your best to set a good example for your kids. Jesus will applaud your positive influence over others. Imagine the moment you see that neighbor or meet a person from the mission you helped fund. Envision the hug you will feel from your son or daughter. What a crown!

There is more.

The Crown of Life

"Blessed are those who endure when they are tested. When they pass the test, they will receive the crown of life that God has promised to those who love him" (James 1:12 GW).

In the Bible a test is a trial that purifies and prepares the heart. Just as a fire refines precious metal from dross and impurities, a trial purges the heart of the same. One of the psalmists wrote:

> For you, God, tested us;
>   you refined us like silver.
> You brought us into prison
>   and laid burdens on our backs.
> You let people ride over our heads;
>   we went through fire and water,
>   but you brought us to a place of abundance.
>
> (Ps. 66:10–12)

You may feel that your entire life has been a test. In and out of hospitals. In and out of foster homes. In and out of treatment centers. In and out of chemotherapy. In and out of solvency. Yet, through it all you refuse to give up. Christ will bless you.

And to those who long for his coming, he gives . . .

The Crown of Righteousness

"I have done my best in the race, I have run the full distance, and I have kept the faith. And now there is waiting for me the victory prize of being put right with God, which the Lord, the righteous Judge, will give me on that Day—and not only to me, but to all those who wait with love for him to appear" (2 Tim. 4:7–8 GNT).

When my three daughters were pre-K age and under, we lived in a house that had a tall, narrow window adjacent to the front door. At any given time, it was likely to be smudged with fingerprints and nose prints. Denalyn would tell the girls I was on the way home, and they would run to the window and wait. They crammed together side by side by side, excited about and looking forward to my return.

God rewards those who do the same for him—those who are "eagerly waiting for him to come again" (2 Tim. 4:8 GW). Ask the Spirit of God to give you a longing for his coming. You will be crowned in righteousness.

The Crown of Glory

"And when the Chief Shepherd appears, you will receive the crown of glory that will never fade away" (1 Peter 5:4).

Peter was speaking to persecuted Christians. They had suffered much for their faith. He wanted them to see that their sufferings were worthwhile. Paul made the same point. "We have small troubles for a while now, but they are helping us gain an eternal glory that is much greater than the troubles" (2 Cor. 4:17 NCV).

To be crowned in glory, then, is to be crowned in victory: a final, ultimate victory over persecution. Scoffers will be silent, and the martyrs will be honored. Those mocked on earth will be praised in heaven. Those belittled on earth will be crowned in heaven.

Does your family criticize your faith? Don't be discouraged. Your day is coming.

Are you the source of jokes at work? Be patient. Your day is coming.

Are you the only believer in your class? Hang in there. Your day is coming.

Sooner than you can imagine, your Father will bless you.

"Good work! You did your job well" (Matt. 25:23 MSG).

That phrase reminds me of a story Joe Stowell told me about a time he met the president at the White House. Joe was president of Moody Bible Institute at the time. He and a dozen or so other leaders were invited to the White House to meet George W. Bush. They each waited in line for their turn to walk across the room and shake his hand.

While Joe waited, he rehearsed his greeting: "Hello, Mr. President, my name is Joe Stowell, president of Moody Bible Institute in Chicago. . . ." Joe planned to go on to tell the president that they were praying for him.

Finally his turn came. When he reached the president, he extended his hand and began: "Hello, Mr. President, my name is Joe Stowell, president of Moody Bible Institute—"

He got no further. The president smiled, slapped him on the shoulder, and said, "Way to go, Joe." He then turned his attention to the next guest as aides escorted a bewildered Joe away. Later in the day he shared the story with his secretary. By the time he returned to Chicago, she'd ordered a T-shirt and hung it on his chair.

It read, "*Way to go, Joe*"*—George W. Bush.*[3]

When he shared the story, we laughed, and then I offered this thought. "You know, Joe, you'll someday hear similar words from the Supreme Commander of the universe. And they won't be spoken casually or quickly. He will look in your eyes and say, 'Way to go, Joe, you've done well.'"

Such is the promise from the pen of Paul. "God will praise each one of them" (1 Cor. 4:5 NCV). What an incredible sentence. "God will praise each one of them." Not "the best of them" or "a few of them" or "the achievers among them." But God will praise *each* of them.

God does not delegate the job. The angel Michael doesn't hand out the crowns. Moses doesn't speak on behalf of the throne. God himself does the honors.

About ten years after my father's death, I spent a few days with my uncle Billy. Dad and Billy looked alike, laughed alike, talked alike. There were moments that weekend when I almost felt I was talking to my father.

As I was preparing to leave, he walked me to the car and did a fine thing. He reached up (he was short like my father), put his hand on my shoulder, looked me squarely in the eye, and said, "Max, your dad would have been proud of you."

If words are golden, I was a rich man. Only one thing would have been better: to hear the words from my father himself.

God sends "Uncle Billys" our way. He sends those who bear the likeness of the Father to encourage us. How we treasure these people, these friends, teachers, ministers, and neighbors. They remind us of our Father in so many ways. Their words are precious. Only one thing would be better: to hear the words from the Father himself.

That day is coming. God will put a crown on your head and a hand on your shoulder and bless you. "God is fair; he will not forget the work you did and the love you showed for him by helping his people" (Heb. 6:10 NCV).

Each child you hugged, he will praise you for it. Every time you forgave, he will praise you for it. Every penny you offered, truth you taught, prayer you prayed, he will praise you for it. He'll praise you for the day you refused to give in and the season you refused to give up. But most of all, he'll praise you for saying yes to Jesus.

You Will Honor Jesus

Does all this talk about crowns, blessings, and rewards confuse you? After all, isn't Paradise a place where we praise God? Isn't he the one worthy of worship? Shouldn't we crown him rather than he crown us?

You are correct. That is exactly what will happen. Ponder the surprising twist of the reward ceremony.

On the unforgettable day when Patmos became Paradise, the apostle John saw what you and I will see. He saw One who sits on the throne. "Around the throne there were twenty-four other thrones with twenty-four elders sitting on them. They were dressed in white and had golden crowns on their heads" (Rev. 4:4 NCV).

The number twenty-four is double twelve, probably representing the twelve Hebrew tribes and the twelve apostles. The Old Israel and the new covenant. The twenty-four are the proxy presence of all the faithful. Those under the commandments and those under the cross. Those who looked toward the Messiah and those who look back to the Messiah. All are represented. Anyone who has desired to kneel before the throne is there. And since the elders represent us, what they do is what we will do.

> Then the twenty-four elders bow down before the One who sits on the throne, and they worship him who lives forever and ever. They put their crowns down before the throne and say:
>
> "You are worthy, our Lord and God,
> to receive glory and honor and power,
> because you made all things."
>
> (Rev. 4:10–11 NCV)

Yes, there will come a day when you will be crowned. Your Maker will praise what you have done. He will bless you. But he will have hardly finished before you fall on your face and lay your crown at his feet.

How gracious of him to give us a crown. For if he didn't, what would we have to give him? As joyfully as you receive it, you will surrender it. As freely as he gave it, you will offer it.

> Heaven has only one head worthy of a crown. And it's not yours, and it's not mine.

I can't wait to see you there. I want to see the look on your face when you see the look on his. One glance into the eyes of the King and you will know the elders were right. Heaven has only one head worthy of a crown. And it's not yours, and it's not mine.

CHAPTER 9

A Marriage Made in Heaven

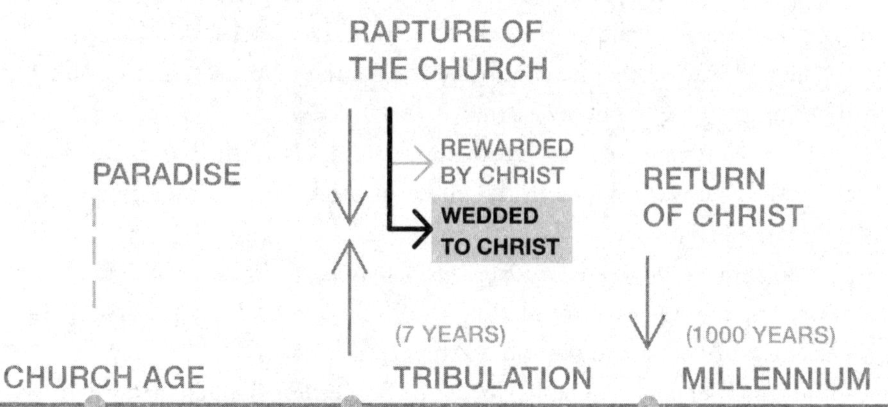

WHAT IS YOUR FAVORITE wedding moment? There are so many from which to choose. From the first downbeat of music to the last crumb of cake at the reception, weddings tug at the heart and fill the photo album. Little boys wear tuxes and carry rings. Misty-eyed moms dab tears with tissues. And when dad gives *her* to *him*, we swallow lumps that go down like tough steak.

We all have favorite wedding moments: candle lighting, groom appearing, rice tossing, cake cutting. The selection is not easy to make.

It may surprise you, then, to learn that one moment is consistently chosen over any other. According to an exhaustive survey by the "Lucado and Associates" research group (conducted over a period of five minutes involving three hallway chats and several good guesses, margin of error 99 percent), there is one event treasured over all others: the entrance of the bride. The organ plays, her mom stands, and the audience jumps to its feet. Even the bridesmaids release a sigh. Why, only minutes before they saw her festooned with curlers and heard her asking for lipstick. But now look at her; from the garland tiara to the satin slippers, she is Cinderella at the ball. We, the peasants, lean forward and gasp. We love the arrival of the bride.

But not nearly as much as Jesus does.

Christ longs to see his bride. His Father has circled the date on the calendar of heaven. The groom is preparing a mansion. Heaven is abuzz with wedding fever. Scripture can't stop talking about the big event!

"The kingdom of heaven is like a certain king who arranged a marriage for his son" (Matt. 22:2 NKJV).

"The kingdom of heaven will be like ten bridesmaids who took their lamps and went to wait for the bridegroom" (Matt. 25:1 NCV).

"[Jesus] died so that he could give the church to himself like a bride in all her beauty . . ." (Eph. 5:27 NCV).

"The Marriage of the Lamb has come; his Wife has made herself ready. She was given a bridal gown of bright and shining linen . . ." (Rev. 19:7–8 MSG).

Look at this language: *marriage, bridesmaids, bridegroom, bride in all her beauty, bridal gown*. Are we reading the Bible or a bridal magazine? Why does Scripture persist in describing the great day as a wedding day?

The answer comes quickly, doesn't it? Something happens at a wedding that happens on no other day, in no other event. The intimacy, romance, physical union, complete surrender. Our union with Jesus is not one of master/slave or creator/created. It is husband/wife. Our arrival in heaven is understood not as a takeover, merger, or amalgamation, but as a wedding between Christ and his bride, the church.

"Let us be glad and rejoice and give Him glory, for the marriage of the Lamb has come, and His wife has made herself ready." And to her it was

> granted to be arrayed in fine linen, clean and bright, for the fine linen is the righteous acts of the saints.
>
> Then he said to me, "Write: 'Blessed are those who are called to the marriage supper of the Lamb!'" And he said to me, "These are the true sayings of God." (Rev. 19:7–9 NKJV)

Plans are underway for a heavenly wedding. The groom is Christ. The bride is the church. By that point we will have been raptured from earth and rewarded by Christ. All the wood, hay, and stubble will have burned away. Only our righteous acts will remain. The next event will be our wedding.

Ancient weddings consisted of two parts: a private and a public celebration. In the private event, the servants of the father of the groom would lead the bride to the prepared house. When all was ready, the father of the bride would place her hand in that of his soon-to-be son. After the private ceremony, the public marriage supper would begin.

Our wedding program will mirror that one. At the rapture we will be led into the presence of Jesus in Paradise. Sometime after the *bēma*-seat ceremony, we will be married to Jesus. When we return with Christ to earth, we will be his wife (Rev. 19:7) and wear the regalia of a bride, "arrayed in fine linen, clean and bright" (Rev. 19:8 NKJV). Our wedding supper will be the millennium. In New Testament times the length and cost of the supper was determined by the wealth of the father. Our Father, whose wealth knows no limits, will celebrate our union with the Son for a thousand years.

> Our wedding supper will be the millennium.

Jesus Woos and Wins His Bride

In the days of Jesus, it fell to the groom to pursue the bride. She might glance as he passed by, she might smile as he turned, but any initiative for marriage was always taken by the groom. As much as she might long for him, she had no hope of a wedding unless he took the first step.

Neither do we. Even if we had the charm to entice heaven, we don't know the phone number. If we have any hope of standing at the altar, God must make the call. And he did! He took the first step. He left his house and came to ours. "It is not our love for God; it is God's love for us. He sent his Son to die in our place to take away our sins" (1 John 4:10 NCV).

Jesus is romancing us. Can he exist without us? Of course, but he doesn't want to. He is smitten, captivated, head-over-heels enchanted with us. He is going to do whatever it takes to win our affection.

I write these words on August 8. Today is my forty-second wedding anniversary. These thoughts about our marriage to Jesus stir memories of mine to Denalyn. I was twenty-five years old, serving a church in Miami, Florida, and happened to be standing in front of the congregation when she entered the back door of the sanctuary on a Sunday morning. Thanks to the summer sun falling through the stained glass, the room was colorful and bright. Thanks to her entrance, the room was made brighter. I lost my place in my sermon and began to lose my heart. Two urgent questions formulated in my mind: "Who is she?" and "How can I get to know her?"

I came to learn her name was Denalyn, she could sing like an angel, and she was twenty-three, a schoolteacher, and, hallelujah, single and unattached. Over the next few weeks, I came to know more about her. She was kind, funny, a friend to the down-and-out.

She had no interest in me, so I set out to change her mind. I called her to chat. I wrote her a few notes. I complimented her hair. I asked her on a date. It took some time, but I eventually was told she had an eye for you-know-who.

At a certain point the question of "who" was eclipsed by "how." How can we have a relationship? The answer came in the form of long walks, talks, a few candlelight dinners, and romantic words. We shared stories of our past, dreams of our future. We kissed. Within a few months, I found myself standing in a jewelry store on a street called Miracle Mile; a miracle indeed, for I'd assumed Max marrying Denalyn was a mile out of my reach. I bought the ring, gave it to her, and a life together began.

Jesus has done more—oh, so much more to woo his bride.

In the first century the groom was required to give money to the father of the bride.[1] The measure of the groom's love was seen in the price he was willing to pay. The measure of Jesus' love is seen in the same.

"You were bought, not with something that ruins like gold or silver, but with the precious blood of Christ, who was like a pure and perfect lamb" (1 Peter 1:18–19 NCV).

"You do not belong to yourselves, because you were bought by God for a price" (1 Cor. 6:19–20 NCV).

Do you want to know how much you matter to Jesus? Find your answer in the blood on the cross. He'd rather die than have heaven without you. So, he did.

Which takes me back to our opening question. *What is your favorite wedding moment?* Most people select the moment they see the bride. My answer is the moment the *groom* sees his bride.

As the wedding officiant, I've waited backstage with him. By this point his shirt is sweat soaked. He tugs on his collar. He licks his dry lips. His groomsmen had jokingly told him to escape, and he may have given the idea serious thought. But now here he stands and here she comes. When he sees her, I sneak a peek at him. His eyes widen. His smile broadens. He takes a deep breath. And I can read his thoughts: *I wouldn't be anywhere else.*

Such will be the thoughts of Jesus when he sees his church. His redeemed saints. His children. His bride. The family for whom he died. The saints with whom he will reign. Clothed in pure grace. From the wreath in her hair to the clouds at her feet, she is royal; she is his princess. "As a man rejoices over his new wife, so your God will rejoice over you" (Isa. 62:5 NCV).

Now That You Are Engaged

In the ancient Jewish world, engagement vows were so binding that the relationship could be broken only by divorce. Even though the couple dwelt in different locations, and even though they had yet to physically consummate the marriage, they were regarded as husband and wife.

The bride-to-be wore a veil when she stepped out of her house to indicate that she was out of circulation. She underwent a purifying bath called a mikvah. The ceremony set her apart for her husband.

Paul invites us to a mikvah of our own, "the washing of water with the word" (Eph. 5:26 NASB). The word for "water" in this passage is specific to rainwater. Not well water or bathwater but the pure shower that comes

Do you want to know how much you matter to Jesus? Find your answer in the blood on the cross. He'd rather die than have heaven without you. So, he did.

from heaven. As you receive his word, he is cleansing you with spring rains. He washes out the old ways and dirt and prepares you for himself.

And, as he prepares us for his place, he prepares a place for us. Jesus, a Jewish man in Jewish culture, had this in mind when he promised, "In My Father's house are many mansions; if it were not so, I would have told you. I go to prepare a place for you. And if I go and prepare a place for you, I will come again and receive you to Myself; that where I am, there you may be also" (John 14:2–3 NKJV).

During the time of preparation, the groom would return to his father's house and prepare a bridal chamber. Zola Levitt explained:

> This was a complex undertaking for the bridegroom. He would build a separate building on his father's property or decorate a room in his father's house. The bridal chamber had to be beautiful . . . one doesn't just honeymoon anywhere. . . . This construction project would take the better part of a year . . . and the father of the groom would be the judge of when it was finished.[2]

In like manner, our heavenly Father will judge when the heavenly chamber is finished. "But of that day and hour no one knows, not even the angels of heaven, but My Father only" (Matt. 24:36 NKJV).

The apostle John caught a glimpse of our next home when the angel took him, as John described it, "to a great, high mountain, and showed me the holy city Jerusalem coming down out of heaven from God, having the glory of God, its radiance like a most rare jewel, like a jasper, clear as crystal" (Rev. 21:10–11 ESV).

This is the city that awaits us after the millennium. "When he measured it, he found it was a square, as wide as it was long. In fact, its length and width and height were each 1,400 miles" (Rev. 21:16 NLT).

Just as Jesus said, his Father's house will have many rooms, and there will be plenty of room for every person of faith who ever lived.

Can't you picture Jesus at work? Construction is no chore; it is a privilege. The work is no burden; it is an opportunity. And with every swing of the hammer and cut of the saw, he's dreaming of the day he brings his bride to his house and carries her over the threshold.

Do you see how your groom loves you? Rest in his love. He will not spurn you as others have. His love is not fickle; his devotion is not fragile. You need do only one thing: "aim at what is in heaven. . . . Think only about the things in heaven" (Col. 3:1–2 ICB).

I'm the dad of three married daughters. I watched their worlds change the days they became engaged. It was all hands on deck. What dress will we buy? Which guests will we invite? What food will we serve? How much will this cost? (I think I was the only one asking that last question.)

Let your heavenly wedding day consume your thoughts. No groom has ever sacrificed more than yours. No groom has gone to greater lengths, journeyed a greater distance, or paid a greater price. No groom has done more to win his bride than Jesus has done to win his church.

He has treated us appropriately, affectionately, respectfully. He has never forced himself upon us. He has never misled or mistreated us. In his proposal, he poured out his heart. On the cross, he poured out his blood.

Our groom has done for us what we could never have done for ourselves. He has qualified us, purified us, sanctified us. He died and rose for us. Never has a groom done more for his bride.

And never has a bride been more unworthy of a groom. He has all authority. We have only what he allows. We tend to forget him, neglect him, behave as if we aren't engaged to him. Yet he refuses to turn away. Just the opposite. He invites us to imagine the moment in which he announces, "I, Jesus, take you, sinner, to be my bride. I covenant before God to be your companion for all eternity. I give you my heart, my home, and my love. We are one forever."

Let your heavenly wedding day consume your thoughts.

Never has there been, never will there be, a wedding like our wedding in heaven. Angels will hover above us. Our praise will well up within us. We will witness the end of this age and the beginning of the next. Sin and death? No more. Tears and fears? No more. Disease and debt, guilt and regret, addictions and afflictions, wars and rage? No more. Not in God's house.

What a wedding. Contemplate it. Ponder it. Set your heart upon it. Let your wedding day define the way you live on this day.

You are engaged, set apart, called out, a holy bride. You've already given your hand to be married. Don't settle for one-night stands in sleazy

No groom has gone to greater lengths, journeyed a greater distance, or paid a greater price. No groom has done more to win his bride than Jesus has done to win his church.

motels. You belong to him. Moreover, he wants to see you more than you want to see him. He has set his sights on you. He died to save you, and he lives to receive you. "He can bring you before his glory without any wrong in you and can give you great joy" (Jude v. 24 NCV).

Some years ago our church studied the wedding celebration of heaven. What better way to conclude the sermon, I thought, than to invite the bride of Christ to walk down the center aisle. We recruited a volunteer, dressed her in a wedding gown and veil. At the appropriate time, I signaled for the music to start and the bride to begin her walk. She did—she walked smack-dab into the back pew. I don't know how I expected her to do anything else; the veil covered her face.

We promptly sent someone to guide her to the altar, just as God long ago sent his Spirit to accompany us. He knows a veil blocks our vision. He knows we trip and fall. But still he calls us his own. He calls us his bride. And something tells me that he will cite the appearance of the bride as the highlight of the wedding.

CHAPTER 10

After the Saints Go Marching In

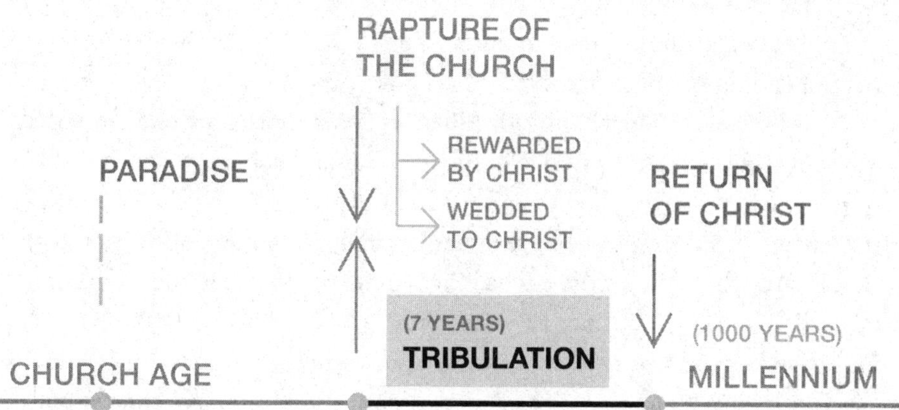

HIGH SCHOOL MAX WAS A MESS. I would not have wanted my daughters to go on a date with the teenage version of their father. I was disrespectful to my parents, dishonest with my school administrators, and a hypocrite in my faith.

My older brother and I made an art form of carousing, drinking, and nightclubbing. He arranged a fake ID for me, showed me where to buy beer, and taught me how to hide our activities from our parents.

But our father knew. Dad was raised in the world of alcohol. His father was a drinker. Several of my aunts and uncles battled alcohol addiction. He was not fooled. He caught and disciplined us more than once. He grounded us, took away the car keys, gave us extra chores.

Nothing worked—until he gave the ultimatum. It came on a Saturday morning, most likely the final straw from a Friday night of intoxication. He sat my brother and me on the couch in our living room. He was not angry as much as matter-of-fact. He foretold the consequence of our folly and how he would not interrupt it.

"Sooner or later you are going to get caught by the law. You will get pulled over for drinking. You'll get arrested for being underaged at a bar. You will end up in jail. The sheriff will call me. He'll ask me to come and bail you out. Sons, here is what you need to know. I will not come for you. I will not vouch for you. I will not put up the money to release you. I will leave you in jail."

The ultimatum was less a threat and more a fact. He was not pretending. He wasn't bluffing. He was earnest and honest. "You stay on this path? Here is where you will end up."

He got my attention.

That conversation comes to mind when I read what the Bible says about an impending season of trouble.

To be clear, God has not destined us for a disastrous end. Just the opposite. He beckons us to live in his splendor and enjoy him forever. "He is not willing that any should perish, and he is giving more time for sinners to repent" (2 Peter 3:9 TLB). He issues his invitation moment by moment. Each sunrise, each starlit night, each grace-kissed blessing. Through nature. Through Scripture. Even the breath in our lungs serves to remind us of God's goodness and our dependence on him.

Yet people reject the offer of God. They tell him to leave them alone. They are willingly wicked and want nothing to do with the whole idea of sin and salvation.

This rejection incurs profound consequences. Just as my earthly father loved us enough to be honest, our heavenly Father loves us enough to be the same. Of course, my dad could only anticipate the outcome. Our heavenly Father can see it. And what he sees is disturbing.

The apostle Paul described this tribulation in detail when he wrote to a church in Thessalonica.

The Day of the Lord

> Brothers and sisters, we have something to say about the coming of our Lord Jesus Christ and the time when we will meet together with him. Do not become easily upset in your thinking or afraid if you hear that the day of the Lord has already come. Someone may have said this in a prophecy or in a message or in a letter as if it came from us. (2 Thess. 2:1–2 NCV)

The Thessalonian Christians were nervous. They were concerned they were living in the "day of the Lord," a biblical term that often points forward to the tribulation. You and I are living in the "day of grace." We endure the consequence of sin but not the direct outpouring of God's wrath. The people of Noah's day felt it. The citizens of Sodom and Gomorrah experienced it. The Egyptians under the pharaoh did as well.

We don't because Jesus Christ received the wrath of God in our place. He cried out, "My God, my God, why have you forsaken me?" (Matt. 27:46 ESV) so we won't have to do so.

The "day of the Lord" is a phrase for judgment. It appears many times in Scripture to refer to the wrath of God. In this case Paul used it twice to refer to a day after "the turning away from God happens and the Man of Evil, who is on his way to hell, appears. He will be against and put himself above any so-called god or anything that people worship. And that Man of Evil will even go into God's Temple and sit there and say that he is God" (2 Thess. 2:3–4 NCV).

Paul was speaking about the Antichrist and his blasphemous act of demanding to be worshiped in the temple. (This presupposes the reconstruction of the temple on the Temple Mount.) In this context the "day of the Lord" is the seven-year period during which God will allow the God-rejectors to feel the full consequences of their rebellion.

A Day of Indifference

The tribulation will begin at some point after the rapture. In an event that will stun the planet, Jesus will descend with a shout and rescue his children from the coming wrath. From one second to the next, families will be missing relatives and offices will be absent workers. Graveyards will be pockmarked with open graves. Hospital staffs will have no explanation for the suddenly vacant beds. School principals won't know what happened to the teachers and students who were there one moment, gone the next.

One might assume the "unraptured" would see the common denominator of the missing people. Each one believed in Jesus. Their skin tones were different. Their heart languages were different. Their political persuasions, nationalities, and income levels were different. But they had this in common: they trusted Jesus Christ for salvation.

We would expect the earthbound to find Bibles and read them, find audio sermons and listen to them, find Christian books and study them. Many won't.

Jesus said, "The love of many will grow cold" (Matt. 24:12 NKJV). Rather than turn to God because of the rapture, people will turn away from God. How could this be? How could they be untouched and unmoved by the most dramatic evacuation in history? Paul placed the blame at the feet of a culprit he called the "Man of Evil" (2 Thess. 2:4 NCV).

What happens to society when millions, maybe billions, of taxpaying, hardworking, God-seeking people suddenly vanish? Who will take up the slack? Who will step into the vacuum? Who will explain their disappearance? Who will stem the sudden tidal wave of fear that will sweep the globe?

The Man of Evil will. He is the Antichrist. With flowing oratory and satanic power, he will offer easy solutions and make exorbitant promises.

Chuck Swindoll offered this summary:

> This man will emerge after the rapture, probably to calm the chaotic waters troubled by the unexplained departure of so many Christians. He will be primed and ready to speak. He will stand before not only a nation but a world and will win their approval. Like Hitler, he will emerge on a scene of such political and economic chaos that people will see him as a man of vision, with pragmatic answers and power to unite the world.[1]

We've never seen anyone like him. He will have no moral compass, no conscience, no sense of right and wrong, no regard for God or people. "He will be against and put himself above any so-called god or anything that

We would expect the earthbound to find Bibles and read them, find audio sermons and listen to them, find Christian books and study them. Many won't.

people worship. And that Man of Evil will even go into God's Temple and sit there and say that he is God" (2 Thess. 2:4 NCV).

If that weren't bad enough, heaven will not restrain him. As Paul wrote, "The secret power of evil is already working in the world, but there is one who is stopping that power. And he will continue to stop it until he is taken out of the way" (2 Thess. 2:7 NCV). God currently keeps evil on a short leash. But in the tribulation, God will let people feel the consequences of their rebellion.

Satan is waiting on the rapture. He is waiting for the Shepherd to lead his flock to safe pasture. Once he and they are gone, the wolf will appear at the gate. Satan will enter the body of the Antichrist just as he entered the body of Judas (John 13:27). God will click the countdown clock, and the final seven years will begin.

Yes, our current days are dark and difficult, but without the power of the Spirit and the influence of the church, the world would be in freefall. So, what will happen when the Spirit's influence through the church is removed?

The Spirit inspired Paul to describe it: "The Man of Evil will come by the power of Satan. He will have great power, and he will do many different false miracles, signs, and wonders. He will use every kind of evil to trick those who are lost. They will die, because they refused to love the truth. (If they loved the truth, they would be saved)" (2 Thess. 2:9–10 NCV).

The Antichrist will conjure some false narrative about the missing believers. He will convince people to stop thinking about them and their Savior and instead give worship to him. And he will succeed.

Amazing. They will have witnessed a miracle second only to the resurrection of Jesus, and they will ignore it. Consequently, the day of grace will become the day of the Lord.

The book of Revelation details the horror. The horsemen will go out to conquer and make war (Rev. 6:1–2). Peace will be taken from the earth. A great many people will be killed (vv. 3–4). Widespread famine and inflation will cause further disruption and death (vv. 5–6). One-fourth of all people will perish (vv. 7–8). Individuals who turn to Christ will become martyrs for their faith (vv. 9–11). An earthquake will drive people into hiding (vv. 12–17). A third of the sun, moon, and stars will be darkened (8:12). The sun will scorch people with fire and fierce heat (16:8–9).

It is no wonder that Jesus declared, "This is going to be trouble on a scale beyond what the world has ever seen, or will see again" (Matt. 24:21 MSG).

A Day of Decision

You might be wondering, *Why should I care about the tribulation? I'll be raptured. I'll be with Jesus. Why does this matter to me?*

Simple. It matters to God. The Bible has at least thirty-six different names for it.[2] The majority of the book of Revelation describes it. Jesus dedicated his final sermon—the Olivet Discourse*—to provide an explanation of it. The tribulation matters to God. It should matter to us.

Though terrible, the tribulation is instructive.

It reminds us that *God hates sin*. He hates what turns people away from him and into violent, depraved, self-centered creatures.

It reminds us that *Satan is a deceiver.* He's lied since the beginning and will lie until the end. He's allergic to the truth. He knows how to dazzle with the promise of peace and the appearance of power. He knows how to control people so they will worship him, not God. For a time during the tribulation, the earthbound will do just that.

There is another reason for understanding the tribulation. *You might experience it.* This is not as far-fetched as you might think. Are you keeping Christ at arm's length? If so, God is doing for you what my father did for my brother and me. He is spelling out the facts. He is describing the consequences. Love does this. Love tells you where the road of disobedience takes you. My father did not want me to go to jail. It was not his desire that I be locked up with ruffians and hoodlums. Yet he left the decision with me.

God has left the decision with you. The tribulation is not your intended destiny. You do not want to be here when the Restrainer is removed and evil runs rampant.

> The tribulation matters to God. It should matter to us.

Say yes before the night comes.

There is one final reason for us to ponder the tribulation. It is possible that these words, written

* Please see Bonus Material from Max, p. 187 for additional information on the Olivet Discourse.

before the rapture, will be read when the church is gone and the chaos has begun. You may be among those who are left behind. If such is the case and you come across this message in a time of tribulation, hear the words of Jesus: "He who endures to the end shall be saved" (Matt. 24:13 NKJV).

> Love tells you where the road of disobedience takes you.

This trouble, while terrible, is temporary. Turn to Christ, trust in Christ, look for Christ.

He is coming soon. We, the church, will be with him.

And the new era of peace, his true peace, will begin.

God has left the decision with you. The tribulation is not your intended destiny. You do not want to be here when the Restrainer is removed and evil runs rampant.

CHAPTER 11

Now That the Chaos Has Come

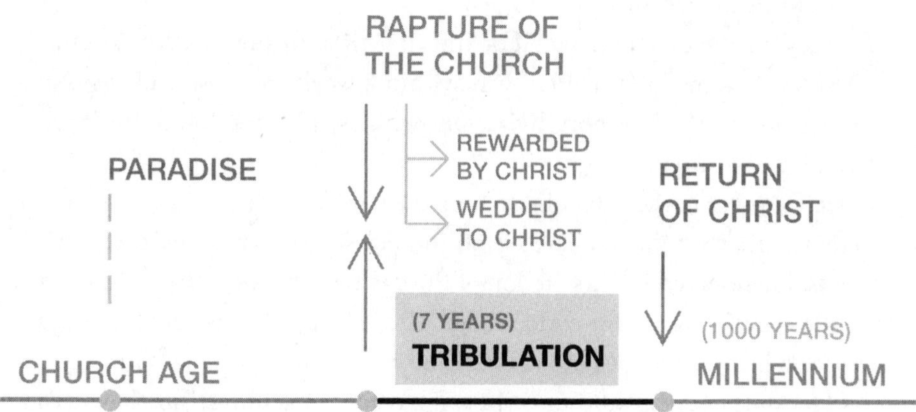

WHAT WILL LIFE BE LIKE after the rapture?

All over the world people will begin the day like any day—breakfast, work, school, exercise. Nothing will happen that would cause anyone to expect anything other than another normal pattern of events. People will scurry and hurry about; parties will be hosted, assignments will be completed, flights will be boarded. Then, in a moment like none ever seen, perhaps billions of people will disappear. In a flash. In a moment. In a nanosecond. Gone. Just like that.

Conversations will stop midsentence. A teacher will look up from her desk to see her class half-empty. With no riders, bicycles will tumble. With no pilots, planes will crash. With no drivers, boats will run onto the shore. It will be the day the world changes forever.

Imagine the global disruption, the confusion, the panic.

It might look something like this.

The Vanishing

The alarm on Jeff's phone went off as it did every morning, way too early to suit him. Was it 6:30 already? He hit the snooze button. But he knew better than to doze off. The English lit exam would begin promptly at 8:00 a.m. He needed every available minute to complete the test. No way could he be late. He dragged himself upright and sat on the edge of the bed. One redeeming thought lifted his spirits.

"This is the last one."

He chuckled at the idea. "For the first time in my life, final exams mean *final* exams." Graduation was within a week. No more college. No more schoolwork. No more living on pennies. He stood and lumbered toward the bathroom.

Jeff was not in the habit of watching the news in the morning. Listening to music, maybe. But no TV, no online newscasts. He didn't even read emails. He reserved his first action of the day for a cup of coffee. Always at the same Let's Brew This coffee shop. Always a double-shot latte. Always served to him by the love of his life, Emily.

Her shift began at 5:00 a.m. She was a year behind him at Northwestern University, and she was always on his mind. His plan that morning was simple. Get dressed. Go to the coffee shop. Give Emily a kiss, and plant himself in a booth and study. He was dressed and down the stairs within fifteen minutes.

That's when he saw the chaos. The sun shed enough light on the May morning to display a street in pandemonium. Cars were stopped in the middle of the road. Some had driven onto the sidewalk and into buildings.

Doors were open. The sound of beeping signals was everywhere. Voices were calling names from all directions.

"John!"

"Elizabeth!"

"Joe and Nathan, where are you?"

A cry from behind jolted Jeff. "Have you seen my children?"

He turned to a panic-stricken mom. "They were in the back seat. I don't know where they are!"

She didn't give Jeff time to answer. She dashed down the street calling their names.

He gathered himself enough to run the one block to the coffee shop. He opened the door to the sight of people standing and staring at TV screens. No one was drinking coffee. No one was serving coffee. He worked his way through the crowd to the counter and looked for Emily. She wasn't there.

"Where's Emily?" he asked her coworker.

"I don't know, Daniel. She was here and . . . then she wasn't."

He felt his heart race. His thoughts were moving so fast he didn't know which one to think.

What is happening?

Where is Emily?

Is this an attack? An abduction?

For the first time he lifted his eyes toward the television. A reporter was standing in the middle of Times Square.

"There is no explanation!" he said. "People are gone."

The report shifted to Washington. A journalist standing in front of the White House stated flatly, "No word. The press secretary has yet to say anything."

Jeff watched for ten minutes. The story was the same everywhere: Beijing, Buenos Aires, Honolulu, and Chicago. *Chicago?* That's where Jeff was. The correspondent stood on Clark Street next to the university and attempted to do what no one could do—explain the sudden disappearance of people. He stopped a student and placed a microphone in her tear-streaked face. "My best friend and I were on a jog. She was with me. I turned to say something and—"

Jeff couldn't bear to watch. He didn't know where to go. But he knew he didn't want to stay. He ran back down the street and up the stairs to his apartment. He closed the door and plopped down on the couch. He watched TV for an hour, maybe two, then turned it off. He was in a daze.

That's when he recalled the box. He opened his closet, the only closet in his efficiency apartment. The wooden box sat on the shelf over his clothing. He took it down and carried it back to the couch.

The letter was still in the envelope. The envelope was taped to the top of the box. It bore his name, hand-scrawled in his granddad's almost illegible handwriting. "Jeff Jacob Harrison."

No address. None was needed. It and the box had been delivered in person.

He removed the letter and read the opening line, "My precious, precious grandson."

Jeff's parents had died in a car crash when he was sixteen years of age. He moved in with Charles and Maggie, his maternal grandparents. If anyone could salvage a broken heart, they could. Charles was an old-fashioned doctor in a small Iowa town. He tried to retire, but people never quite let him. He was still delivering babies and checking on patients when he was eighty years old.

They lived on a few acres outside the Quad Cities. Jeff had been raised in Chicago. The adjustment to rural life was more than he could handle at first. It turned out to be exactly what he needed. He had cousins down the road. He made friends and went to the small school. Life was slower. Charles and Maggie showed Jeff every possible kindness. They listened when he wanted to talk. They gave him space when he needed to be quiet.

In time he began to breathe deeper and think about his future. Thanks to them, he weathered the storm.

Jeff cherished everything about Charles and Maggie, everything but their faith. Jeff's dad had rejected spirituality. He was Jewish but in name only. He was a good man, hard worker, self-made, and successful. He needed no Savior. Those were the exact words Daniel overheard him say to his mom one Sunday morning when their conversation got heated. She asked him, for the umpteenth time, to go to church with her. He scoffed at the thought and made the "Savior" remark. As far as Jeff knew, she never asked him again.

As a boy, Jeff tagged along with his mom and went to Sunday school. But when given the chance to make a choice, he imitated his father.

When his grandparents went to church, he refused to go. They chose not to force him. When they brought up the subject, he politely declined to discuss it.

He loved them.

They loved him.

But he refused to believe.

His father's mantra became his own. "I need no Savior."

Jeff met Emily during the first week of his senior year at Northwestern. The campus was in a festive mood. The patrons at the Blue Cat Bar were especially rowdy. Lots of beer was charged to lots of parents' credit cards. Jeff drank his share and, consequently, was especially spunky when he saw this petite blonde from Baton Rouge. They would later laugh at his opening line.

"My name is Jeff, and I'm ready for a new life. Can I start it with you?"

Really, really hokey. But, given the beer and the atmosphere, it was forgivable. Emily laughed, and that's how their relationship began. Within a month he took her to meet his grandparents. By Thanksgiving she'd begun calling them Pop and Memaw, just like Jeff did.

Driving back to Chicago after Thanksgiving, Emily was uncharacteristically quiet. Jeff asked about it.

"Memaw talked to me about Jesus," she said.

Jeff sighed. "I knew that would happen sooner or later. I'll tell her to lay off."

"No, Jeff. I want to know. In fact, I already know."

She shared a part of her life that they had yet to discuss. She was a Christian. She was eight years old when she made the decision in a Bible class.

"Jeff, when I spoke to your Memaw, I felt again what I felt back then. She told me I was feeling the Holy Spirit. That he had never left me." Jeff started to quip something clever but saw a tear in her eye. So he said nothing.

They continued to date. They agreed not to discuss religion. But he noticed she began to carry a Bible. He also noticed she began to carry a sense of peace.

No time was that peace more evident than when his grandfather died. He passed away in December on a Sunday afternoon. Memaw thought he was napping. He wasn't; he was gone.

The funeral was held at the community church. Jeff found it difficult to focus. The loss of his grandfather triggered memories of his parents' funeral. He wept through the service.

The family gathered afterward at Maggie's house. All the cousins. A scattering of uncles and aunts. It was a talkative group. Jeff found it a relief, a respite from sadness. He even caught himself laughing at a cousin's story. For a moment he forgot the reason for the event.

After everyone had gone, Maggie asked Jeff and Emily to take a seat. She left and returned with the box. It was wooden. Polished. The lid bore a lockable latch. She handed the box to Jeff. An envelope was taped to the top. His name was scribbled in a doctor's scratch.

Jeff looked at her. "Do you know what this is?"

"I do, Jeff."

A small key fell out as Jeff removed the one-page, handwritten letter from the envelope. He read:

> My precious, precious grandson.
>
> I could not be prouder. You have borne up under more grief than a person should ever have to bear. You have done so with dignity and courage.
>
> The fact that you are reading this means that my spirit is no longer on this earth. My life has been long and rich. I depart with no regrets. I have only one unfinished task. It has to do with you, my Jeff.
>
> Here is what I want you to know. Your salvation was my final offered prayer. Each time I pray I begin and end by asking God to touch your heart. So I know without a doubt that the last prayer I offered in this life concluded with a request for your salvation.
>
> This box you hold contains something that I pray you will never need. I pray you will join your mother, your grandmother, and me in believing in Jesus. With all my heart I do.
>
> But if you don't, there is the possibility you will be alive when Jesus comes for his church. I know you don't like this talk. You think it is folly, antiquated. But please bear with me.
>
> You might be alive on the day everything changes. I mean everything. From one moment to the next, people will vanish. They will disappear. No one will have an explanation.

I want to give you one. Christ came for them. He took them to Paradise to prepare them to be his heavenly bride.

I know you are shaking your head at this. So I'll stop. But I close with a request. You are a man of your word, so I know you will honor it. Do not open this box unless that day happens.

But if that day happens, open it. *For heaven's sake, open it*!

You need to know what's coming. While I can't forecast details, I know this: the times are about to get very dire. Keep the box. Keep the key. And know that I love you.

Jeff handed the note to Emily and turned to Maggie. "I'll know when the time is right to open it?"

Maggie nodded.

Jeff returned the key to the envelope and placed the box on the couch.

He couldn't resist one more question. "Do you know what it contains, Memaw?"

She nodded.

Jeff and Emily drove back to Chicago. They tried to discuss the box, but neither knew what to say. So mysterious. So cryptic. They ended up discussing everything else—the funeral, the family, the cold December weather. Jeff kept his promise, however. The box sat unopened in his apartment closet.

The fall semester came to a close. The spring semester began. Jeff and Emily studied, worked, and welcomed the warm spring weather. They fell more and more in love. Discussions about a future together began to take a serious tone. Life felt normal. Happy. Vibrant.

Until that morning in May.

The Lamb Takes the Scroll

No one knows exactly what life will be like in a post-rapture world. But this much is sure: it will be a shock to global society. While the church is celebrating with Jesus at a reward ceremony and a wedding, the world will be left stunned and confused, attempting to maintain some sort of balance.

People like Jeff will struggle to make sense of it all. If I had the chance to leave a note for someone like him to read, I'd direct that person to one of the great chapters in the Bible, the fifth chapter of Revelation. This power-packed section describes the event that will set the stage for the dystopian condition of the tribulation.

In a vision the apostle John saw Jesus in the throne room of heaven. Jesus was identified as "the Lion of the tribe of Judah" (Rev. 5:5 ESV). John also saw a seven-sealed scroll in the hand of God the Father (Rev. 5:1).

The chief question of the vision has to do with the scroll. John "saw a mighty angel proclaiming in a loud voice, 'Who is worthy to break the seals and open the scroll?' But no one in heaven or on earth or under the earth could open the scroll or even look inside it" (Rev. 5:2–3).

In the first century the only document sealed with seven seals was a last will and testament.[1] The first readers of the vision would have recognized the scroll as an inheritance. The question of the angel was, in fact, "Who is worthy to receive the inheritance of heaven, to be King of the universe?"

The answer? *No one in heaven or on the earth.*

John heard the news, and he began to weep. "I wept and wept because no one was found who was worthy to open the scroll or look inside" (Rev. 5:4).

If no one can open the scroll, then there is no one to inherit the kingdom. John wept at the thought of a kingless cosmos. No triumphant heaven. No hope. No victory. No reason to do anything except weep. Dr. W. A. Criswell wrote:

> John's tears represent the tears of all God's people through all the centuries. They're the tears of Adam and Eve as they view the still form of their dead son Abel and sense the awful consequence of their disobedience. These are all the tears of all the children of Israel in bondage as they cried to God for deliverance from affliction and slavery. They are sobs and tears wrung from the heart and soul of God's people as they've stood beside graves of loved ones and experienced the indescribable heartaches and disappointments of life. Such is the curse that sin has laid upon God's beautiful creation. No wonder John wept so fervently. If no redeemer could be found to remove the curse, it meant God's creation was forever consigned to remain in the hands of Satan.[2]

But then Jesus. "He went and took the scroll from the right hand of him who sat on the throne" (Rev. 5:7).

Jesus marched right up to the Father and did what no one else could do; he lay claim to his inheritance. Jesus, the lion who was a lamb, took the reins of human history. He is the commander, the general, the only authority. He is worthy to open the scroll because he gave his life for the kingdom.

When the residents of heaven saw Jesus take the scroll, they erupted in worship. Hallelujahs everywhere. The four living creatures worshiped. The twenty-four elders worshiped. John heard "the voice of many angels, numbering thousands upon thousands, and ten thousand times ten thousand" (Rev. 5:11).

In a mighty chorus they proclaimed, "Worthy is the Lamb!" (v. 12).

Not everyone rejoiced. Satan would not surrender the earthly kingdom to Christ. Jesus responded to his rebellion with judgments. The judgments served to display his superiority over Satan and offered hard-hearted earth-dwellers a final opportunity to repent. As Jesus opened each seal, a calamity happened. Economies tumbled. Weather raged. People like Jeff faced widespread suffering and turmoil.

Yet, there was also a most unlikely event.

Jews for Jesus

In John's vision he saw four angels ready to unleash the fury of God's judgment. But another angel appeared, calling for a delay. "Wait! Don't harm the land or the sea or the trees until we have placed the seal of God on the foreheads of his servants" (Rev. 7:3 NLT).

Who are these servants? John told us: "Then I heard the number of those who were sealed: 144,000 from all the tribes of Israel" (Rev. 7:4).

John offered two key details about these servants of God. They will be Jewish, and they will be "sealed"; that is, they will be marked, identified as God's chosen ones. Later John tells us the seal means having Jesus' "name and his Father's name written on their foreheads" (Rev. 14:1 NLT). Which names? Adonai? Jehovah? Elohim? We are not told. This much is sure: to be tattooed with God's name in the day of the Antichrist is no small thing. Earlier Jesus gave this promise: "The one who conquers, . . . I will write

Jesus marched right up to the Father and did what no one else could do; he lay claim to his inheritance. Jesus, the lion who was a lamb, took the reins of human history.

on him the name of my God . . . and my own new name" (Rev. 3:12 ESV). These will receive the promise.

This will be a crack battalion of God's servants. Satan will throw his fire and brimstone at them, but they will not be destroyed. Invincible and unassailable. Nor will their work be futile. The description of the 144,000 is followed by the appearance of an innumerable multitude, implying that the work of these Jews will result in a massive harvest of souls.

"After this I looked, and there before me was a great multitude that no one could count, from every nation, tribe, people and language, standing before the throne and before the Lamb. They were wearing white robes and were holding palm branches in their hands" (Rev. 7:9).

This will be the finest hour of the Jewish people. When God told Abraham that his descendants would be a blessing to the world, this event was part of that promise. "All peoples on earth will be blessed through you" (Gen. 12:3). Hearts that were hard toward God will soften at the proclaimed gospel of Jesus, causing an enormous revival, fulfilling the prophecy of Christ: "And this gospel of the kingdom will be preached in the whole world as a testimony to all nations, and then the end will come" (Matt. 24:14).

In addition to the 144,000 Jewish evangelists, two men will proclaim Christ. "I will give power to my two witnesses, and they will prophesy one thousand two hundred and sixty days, clothed in sackcloth" (Rev. 11:3 NKJV). A case can be made that the identity of these two men is Moses and Elijah. One a lawgiver, the other a prophet. They appeared during the transfiguration of Jesus; perhaps they will appear in the tribulation. The witnesses will have power to turn water into blood (Rev. 11:6), duplicating a famous miracle of Moses (Ex. 7:14–24). They will have the power to destroy their enemies with fire (Rev. 11:5), mirroring an event in the life of Elijah (2 Kings 1).

They will declare the justice of God in a world of evil. Midway through the tribulation, they will be killed and their bodies displayed in Jerusalem. But death is no match for the Giver of life. John prophesied that after three and one-half days, "the breath of life from God entered them, and they stood on their feet, and great fear fell on those who saw them" (Rev. 11:11 NKJV). And, as if the dozen sets of 12,000 evangelists and the two resurrected witnesses were not enough, God will release an angel:

> And I saw another angel flying through the heavens, carrying the everlasting Good News to preach to those on earth—to every nation, tribe, language, and people. "Fear God," he shouted, "and extol his greatness. For the time has come when he will sit as Judge. Worship him who made the heaven and the earth, the sea and all its sources." (Rev. 14:6–7 TLB)

This is a full-scale, heaven-born evangelistic crusade! How many souls will be saved? A "multitude that no one could count" (Rev. 7:9). I smile when I read that line. I've been around preachers and evangelists my entire adult life. One thing we learn to do early is take attendance and count baptisms. But on that day no one will be able to tabulate the salvations.

Among them, at least in my imagination, will be young Jeff. Let's close this chapter by closing out his story. You might recall that his girlfriend was a Christ-follower and disappeared at the rapture, and he was left holding a box given to him by his believing grandfather.

It's Not Too Late

Jeff sat on the edge of the couch holding the box in one hand and the key in the other. He looked at the note, then looked out the window at the distant glow of a city on fire. He sighed and reread his grandfather's words. When he came to the lines "From one moment to the next, people will vanish. They will disappear. No one will have an explanation," he whispered to himself, "Pop, how did you know?"

He turned the lock. Inside the box was a large gold cross on a gold chain. A second note was written on a folded sheet from his grandfather's prescription tablet.

> Jeff, now that the chaos has come, this world will turn increasingly dark. Flee to my farm. You'll find provisions for every need.
>
> Please reflect on what you've heard me say since you were young. Jesus Christ is the Lord of this universe. He died for you so that you can live with him forever. Accept his invitation.

> Keep this cross. At some point in the future, the near future, I pray, you will encounter some Jewish evangelists. You will see the name of God on their foreheads. When you see them, think of this letter. The evangelists are the answer to our prayers for you.

Jeff looked at the cross, then the letter. He stuck both in his pocket. There was a day when he would have chalked these words up to his grandpa's foolishness. But now? Not now. Not after what he'd seen.

Just as his grandfather forewarned, the world turned cold and angry. If something bad could happen, it did. The US government, once a beacon of hope, collapsed. The economy gave way to socialism. Pandemics broke out on every continent.

Jeff survived by making his way to his grandparents' acreage. Other than a few neighbors on adjacent farms, he avoided people. The property had a generator, a water well, and a garden. He was able to live off the grid and avoid the calamities.

In the house he came across many copies of the Bible. He began to read. He read and reread about the life of Christ, the cross, and the empty tomb. He read the book of Revelation and recognized he was living it out in real time.

On the day a stranger walked up his path, Jeff immediately knew who he was. Around his neck was the cross of Christ. On his forehead was the name of God. When Jeff saw it, he reached into his pocket, pulled out the cross given to him by his grandfather, and hung it around his own neck.

CHAPTER 12

The Crowns and the Crimson

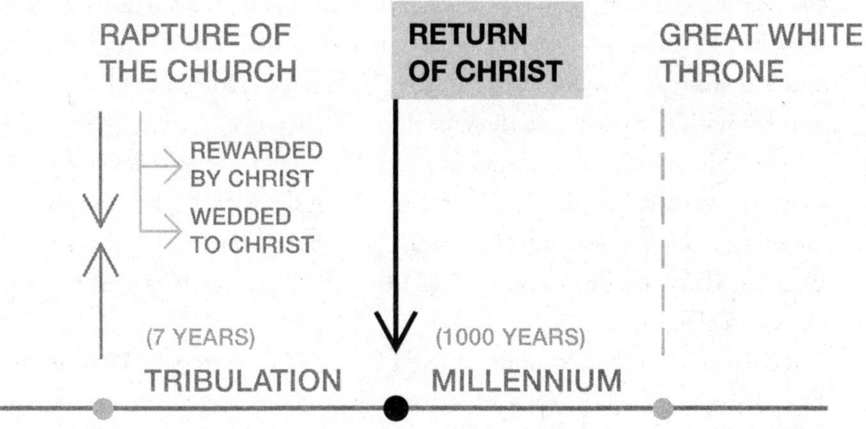

EVERYONE LOVES THE CHRIST in the cradle. The image of baby Jesus in the Bethlehem barn warms our hearts. Each December we recreate the moment on our lawns and beneath our Christmas trees. Stores sell plastic donkeys and wooden mangers. People collect hand-carved images of Mary, Joseph, and the newborn child.

We love the Christ in the cradle.

We are fine with Christ the gentle Messiah. Children sitting on his lap. Sheep gathered around him. The apostle John reclining on his chest. Mary anointing his feet. No one has an issue with a pleasant rabbi who offers sage advice, feeds crowds, and replenishes wine at a wedding.

Christ in the cradle? Wonderful. Christ the kindhearted? Delightful. But Christ the coming King? On a stallion? Roaring out of heaven? Crowned with the crowns of his enemies? On a mission to destroy those who destroy his children?

The world is less familiar with this view of Jesus. Yet this is the Jesus the world will soon see.

Our Coming King

"Now I saw heaven opened, and behold, a white horse. And He who sat on him was called Faithful and True" (Rev. 19:11 NKJV).

With these words the apostle John initiates his eye-popping, cinematic description of the return of Jesus to planet Earth. By this point in history, the church will have been raptured, rewarded by, and wed to Jesus. We will have our glorified bodies. We will be reunited with loved ones we buried and acquainted with heroes we studied. We will no longer see by faith but will see with our own eyes the face of our Redeemer.

By this point the residents of earth will have endured seven years of famines, wars, pandemics, and disarray. An evil ruler will demand worship and defy God. Yet even during apocalyptic disruption, God will save souls. One angel, two witnesses, and 144,000 Jewish evangelists will trigger a global awakening.

Engraved in the Rotunda of the Library of Congress in Washington, DC, are these words: "One God, one law, one element, and one far-off, divine event, to which the whole creation moves."[1] The return of Jesus is the "far-off, divine event." The details, characters, antagonists, heroes, and subplots all arc in this direction. God's story carries us toward a coronation for which all creation longs. "He was supreme in the beginning and—leading the resurrection parade—he is supreme in the end" (Col. 1:18 MSG).

It is the central focus of prophecy and a dominating theme of all Scripture. The prophet Isaiah prayed, "Oh, that You would rend the heavens! That You would come down!" (Isa. 64:1 NKJV). The psalmist agreed:

"Bow down Your heavens, O LORD, and come down; touch the mountains, and they shall smoke" (Ps. 144:5 NKJV). Paul spoke of "the blessed hope and glorious appearing of our great God and Savior Jesus Christ" (Titus 2:13 NKJV).

Scripture gushes with the news of Christ's return like water in full spate. To the depressed disciples Jesus assured, "I will come again" (John 14:3 NKJV). When Jesus ascended, the angel told the witnesses, "[Jesus] will come back in the same way you have seen him go into heaven" (Acts 1:11). Paul referred to "the appearing of our Lord Jesus Christ" (1 Tim. 6:14). Peter affirmed, "The day of the Lord will come" (2 Peter 3:10). Jude announced, "See, the Lord is coming with thousands upon thousands of his holy ones" (Jude v. 14).

As I commented earlier, the second coming is mentioned more than three hundred times in the Bible, an average of once every twenty-five verses.[2]

The second coming is mentioned more than three hundred times in the Bible, an average of once every twenty-five verses.

Just read the way Jesus described it:

> Then, the Arrival of the Son of Man! It will fill the skies—no one will miss it. Unready people all over the world, outsiders to the splendor and power, will raise a huge lament as they watch the Son of Man blazing out of heaven. At that same moment, he'll dispatch his angels with a trumpet-blast summons, pulling in God's chosen from the four winds, from pole to pole. (Matt. 24:30–31 MSG)

Jesus packs the paragraph with exclamation points and lightning bolts. Look at these phrases: "fill the skies," "huge lament," "Son of Man blazing." It's like every major event merged into one moment. The Indian Ocean tsunami and the celebration of V-day. One part black plague, another part blue ribbon. The Berlin Wall collapses, Mount Vesuvius erupts, the *Enola Gay* drops the bomb, and penicillin is discovered all in one second. Everything good and bad, all that could change does change—and all at once.

John's vision of Christ's return is enough to accelerate your pulse. (If you have a heart condition, please take a nitroglycerin tablet.) "I saw heaven opened" (Rev. 19:11 NCV). As if the sky were blue tissue, hands pulled it apart. When they did, John saw Jesus on a white horse. First-century readers knew that conquering kings returned from battle on a white stallion. Jesus will return in absolute victory.

He will appear wearing "many crowns" (Rev. 19:12). In ancient times when a king conquered an enemy, he would wear the crown of the defeated king. Jesus will descend wearing all the diadems of all would-be kings. How many crowns did Satan wear in Revelation 12? Seven. How many crowns did the Antichrist wear in Revelation 13? Ten. In the end Satan will have no crowns. The Antichrist will have no crowns. The demons will have no crowns. Dictators and oligarchs will have no crowns. The great un-crowning. Only Christ will be crowned.

He will descend upon the Mount of Olives, the very place from which he ascended into heaven. This is the prophecy from Zechariah and the promise of the angel. Zechariah foretold, "And in that day His feet will stand on the Mount of Olives" (Zech. 14:4 NKJV). After Jesus ascended from the Mount of Olives, the angel told the disciples Jesus "will come back in the same way you have seen him go" (Acts 1:11).

His eyes will appear like a "flame of fire" (Rev. 19:12 NKJV). He will see everything. No corner of the earth and no corner of the heart will be hidden from his view. He will wear a "robe dipped in blood" (Rev. 19:13 NKJV). The crimson hue is a proof of purchase, a bill of sale, a reminder that "Christ bought us with His blood" (Gal. 3:13 NLV). He has every right to inherit the kingdom. He paid for us. He is the "Lamb slain from the foundation of the world" (Rev. 13:8 Phillips).

White horse. Countless crowns. Blazing eyes. Bloody robe. This is not your baby Jesus meek and mild. This is your King Jesus, mighty and riled. Look at the military language: "He judges and makes war" (Rev. 19:11 NCV). "Out of the rider's mouth comes a sharp sword that he will use to defeat the nations" (Rev. 19:15 NCV).

Our Conquering King

Who are these nations, and what have they done to incur this divine blitzkrieg? They are brazenly evil renegades. They have shaken a fist at Jesus. They have set their hearts against God and against the kingdom.

The epistle of Jude adds clarity to this event: "Behold, the Lord comes with ten thousands of His saints, to execute judgment on all, to convict all who are ungodly among them of all their ungodly deeds which they have committed in an ungodly way, and of all the harsh things which ungodly sinners have spoken against Him" (Jude vv. 14–15 NKJV).

The word *ungodly* appears four times. Jesus will deal with those who defied him.

These people could have repented prior to the tribulation. God spoke through miracles of the universe and the words of Scripture.

The rebels could have repented after the rapture. But the spectacular sign of an extracted church did not soften their hearts.

The insurgents could have repented at any point during the seven years of calamity, but they "neither repented of the works of their own hands nor ceased to worship evil powers and idols. . . . Neither did they repent of their murders, their sorceries, their sexual sins, nor of their thieving" (Rev. 9:20–21 PHILLIPS). Surely they heard the message of the 144,000 evangelists. Certainly they knew about the two witnesses and the soaring angel who declared the gospel. Great multitudes heard and believed, but these heard and ignored.

Who are these anarchists? They are the kings of the world who have gathered for the battle of Armageddon (Rev. 16:12–16). They have come to make war with Jesus (Rev. 17:14). "And I saw the beast, the kings of the earth, and their armies, gathered together to make war against Him who sat on the horse and against His army" (Rev. 19:19 NKJV).

Let's be clear. These are not people who want to know Christ but struggle to do so. These are not individuals who seek to follow Jesus but stumble. These are bad-to-the-bone rebels who choose Satan over salvation. They blaspheme God and ravage the innocent. They have bowed a knee to the Antichrist and turned their backs on the living Christ. They have assembled under the ludicrous notion that they are mightier than Jesus.

The King has come to set them straight.

And you will be there to watch him do it. Surprised? If so, let me take you to the verse that bears your name and mine. "And the armies in heaven, clothed in fine linen, white and clean, followed Him on white horses" (Rev. 19:14 NKJV).

That's you. That's me. The bride of Christ. Clothed in wedding garments. Saddle up! We will descend with our King on our stallions.

A gospel song opens with this line: "I want a one-way ticket to heaven. I won't be back this way no more."[3] I appreciate the sentiment, but the verse is inaccurate. You don't have a one-way ticket to heaven. You have a round-trip ticket that will transport you to heaven for your rewards and wedding and then return you to earth for the final battle. "The Lord comes with ten thousands of His saints" (Jude v. 14 NKJV).

But if you are worried about engaging in the conflict, don't be. Though you'll be in the army, you won't fight the enemy. That's the job of our General. With one weapon Jesus Christ will wipe out all who oppose him. They will be "killed by the sword of the One on the horse, the sword that comes from his mouth" (Rev. 19:21 MSG). One word from the mouth of Jesus is all it will take. He once spoke a word to a fig tree and it died, to a storm and it stilled, to a legion of demons and they fled, to a dying slave and he was healed. One word is all it will take to smite the nations.

This will be no extended, protracted war. No volley, no back-and-forth. The victory of Jesus will occur in an instant. He will cast the false prophet and the Antichrist into the lake of fire (Rev. 19:20). God will invite the birds of the air to gorge themselves on the slain. This carnage is called "the supper of the Great God" (Rev. 19:17 NKJV).

And so the tribulation will end, the earth will be purged and made pure, Christ's coronation will begin, and Jesus will live up to the name written on his thigh: "KING OF KINGS AND LORD OF LORDS" (Rev. 19:16).

What are we to do with this striking prophecy? How are we to process it?

I suggest we take it seriously.

Our Compelling King

In May 1942 General Douglas MacArthur made a promise to the people of the Philippines. The general commanded Allied Forces in the South Pacific. After American and Filipino troops were forced to surrender to the invading Japanese army, MacArthur assured the people they would see him again. He had the words "I shall return" printed on leaflets and scattered over the islands. He kept his promise. He came back. By July 1945 the country was liberated. A month later World War II ended.[4]

Christ has done more than drop leaflets. He entered the womb of a Jewish peasant. He walked the dusty trails of our world. He died the death of a sinner yet rose from the tomb a Savior. He repeatedly promised his return. He will descend bearing all crowns and wearing a crimson robe. Christ's second advent will be unlike his first.

The first coming was all about salvation. The second is all about coronation. In his first coming, Jesus Christ came to seek and save. In his second, he will come to rule and reign. In Jesus' first advent, he was falsely judged by evil men. In his second, he will rightly judge evil men. When he first came, his eyes wept at the tomb of Lazarus. When he reappears, his eyes will blaze with fire. Soldiers gave Jesus a crown of thorns. Christ will descend wearing all the crowns of history. People mocked him on his first advent. All will bow before him upon his second.

"At the name of Jesus every knee shall bow in heaven and on earth and under the earth, and every tongue shall confess that Jesus Christ is Lord, to the glory of God the Father" (Phil. 2:10–11 TLB).

The US Census Bureau estimates that 106 billion people have been born since the dawn of humanity.[5] Every single one of them will bow before Jesus.

Who will kneel?

Everyone in *heaven*. Moses, Mary, your grandpa, my big brother, every citizen of Paradise.

Everyone *on the earth*. This includes the countless souls saved and the hard-hearted lost during the tribulation. Demons who prowl the earth will grudgingly show submission. Angels who protect the earth will joyfully kneel.

And everyone *under the earth*. Even hades will have a worship service. The rich man who ignored Lazarus. Judas who betrayed Jesus. Ahab and Jezebel who sought to kill Elijah. And Haman who planned the first holocaust. All will bow before Christ.

This extraordinary thought warrants a straightforward question. Knowing we shall kneel before him on that day, how should we live on this day? Shouldn't his coming stimulate our reverence? Activate our obedience?

An example of our readiness is seen in Arlington National Cemetery. The men and women who guard the Tomb of the Unknown Soldier display a level of unparalleled fidelity. They devote eight hours to the preparation of their uniforms. Gloves are worn wet to improve the grip on the rifle. Shanks are attached to the inside of each shoe so the soldier can click his or her heels.

The sentinel repeats the same walk over and over: twenty-one steps, then a twenty-one second pause, the rifle is shifted to the other shoulder, then twenty-one more steps. He or she repeats this until being relieved at the changing of the guard.

During the summer months the soldier is on duty for thirty minutes. During the winter, sixty minutes. They fulfill their task in the heat of August and the chill of January. The routine never varies, not even at night when the cemetery is closed. When Hurricane Isabel moved through the area in 2003, the soldiers never stopped. Not once. Trees fell and the wind whipped, but they kept their post.

> Knowing we shall kneel before him on that day, how should we live on this day?

They have maintained this vigilance every day of every year since 1921.[6]

Remarkable.

Question: If they can display such allegiance rightly given to unknown, dead soldiers, can we not do the same for our living, coming, ruling King? If these sentries are willing to patrol in honor of those who sacrificed, can't we do even more for our King, who gave the greatest sacrifice? We are members of his battalion. We are enlisted in his regiment. We are returning with him someday. Can we not serve him on this day?

Let me be specific. What can you do today in honor of your King? What kindness can you perform? What offense can you forgive? What temptation can you resist? What gift can you offer? What discipline can you begin? What sacrifice can you make? What act of love can you show?

Let's behave like the people we have been called to be: soldiers in the returning army of the King of kings.

The Christ of the cradle is now the Christ with the crowns. He is coming soon.

CHAPTER 13

God Will Have His Garden

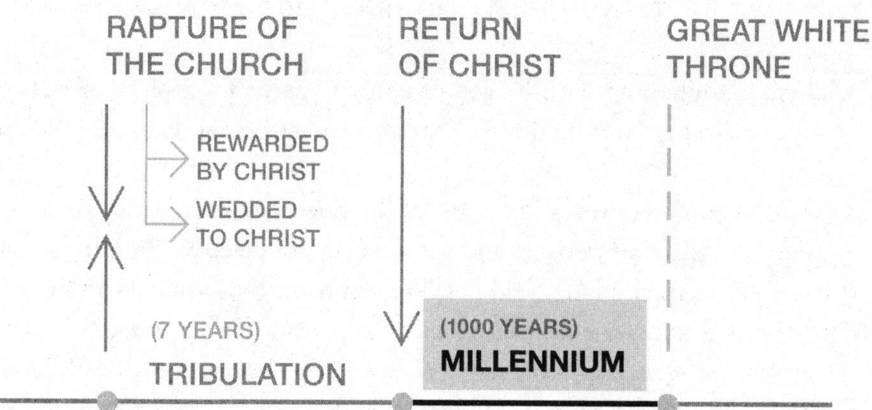

IN SEARCH OF UTOPIA, I drove to Utopia. The trip is a quick and pleasant one. Take Highway 90 westward out of San Antonio, and you'll soon enter the city limits of Utopia, Texas, population 227.

I went to research this chapter. I conversed with about half a dozen folks, each one as friendly as the sky is blue. A couple work in the feed store. Another person runs a gas station. I spoke with two ladies at a restaurant—one a server and the other the owner. All were pleased to offer a response to my question, "How did the town get the name Utopia?" (The answer given with the most confidence: a postmaster made the change in 1880 hoping to attract settlers.)

The word *Utopia* was coined more than five hundred years ago by Thomas More, a Roman Catholic philosopher. It designates a fictional, idyllic society that existed on a remote island somewhere in the Atlantic. Over the centuries the word has come to symbolize a place of perfection, equality, harmony, and prosperity.

That said, I can confidently tell you that Utopia, Texas, is not utopian. No disrespect intended, but the town is far from perfect. A street needed repair. A drought had dried up the Sabinal River. Trees bore blight. A dilapidated double-wide trailer implied the presence of poverty. A couple of longtime residents bemoaned the arrival of newcomers and the skyrocketing price of ranchland.

So Utopia is not Utopia.

Why Our World Is Upside Down

There is something within each of us that yearns for a place of justice, safety, morality, and kindness. Peace on earth, goodwill to all. We are dissatisfied. We crave Utopia.

Will this world ever know it? Will a government someday solve the issues of corruption, crime, and greed so that a place called Utopia will live up to its name? I'm afraid not. We can paint the letters on a sign, but humanity won't create a perfect society. How can I be so certain?

Satan is on the prowl. Satan is not a word for the presence of evil. Satan is the person of evil. He is a real spirit who desires nothing but your misery. "The devil is your enemy, and he goes around like a roaring lion looking for someone to attack and eat" (1 Peter 5:8 ERV).

He deceives, steals, and destroys. If Satan is on the loose, Utopia has no chance.

There is a second reason: *Jesus is unwelcome.* Most of the world wants nothing to do with him. People want the benefits of Jesus. We want kindness, inclusion, forgiveness; we want the blessings of Christ's kingdom.

But a king? An absolute authority? One who has the final say on our lives? That's another matter. Only 39 percent of Americans say they read portions of the Bible multiple times per year. Only 10 percent report daily Bible reading.[1]

Christ, in other words, is rarely consulted. His words are irrelevant to most people. Jesus is unheard of in our homes, schools, even churches.

As it stands, our world is a kingless kingdom. Jesus has all authority over heaven and earth (Matt. 28:18), but insurgents by the billions resist his right to rule. They are a part of hell's coup. The prayer "Thy kingdom come, Thy will be done" (Matt. 6:10 KJV) is being answered in the hearts of believers, but it has yet to be answered fully in society. Consequently, Utopia is still a dream, not a reality.

Satan is on the loose.

Jesus is unwelcome.

And one more—*our rulers are unrighteous.* Sinners govern our world. For every good, righteous, decent person in authority, there are dozens who seek nothing more than self-interest. How can we hope to find Utopia if leaders oppress the weak, embezzle funds, or hide the truth? They, like us, fall short of God's standards. And unrighteous rulers cannot righteously rule.

So what hope do we have? Will this planet ever know a time of abundance and provision? Will this earth forever groan under the weight of sin and the influence of Satan?

When Our World Will Be Right Side Up

A stunning, surprising, and powerful answer is found in the twentieth chapter of the book of Revelation. John foresees a thousand-year period of global peace and prosperity. Satan will be trapped and incarcerated. Jesus will be enthroned and worshiped. And we, the redeemed saints, will fulfill our Edenic commission and reign with him as righteous rulers on the earth.

Revelation 19 describes the return of Jesus and his retinue of saints and angels. He will descend in a fiery fury and decimate the main players of the tribulation: the Beast, the false prophet, and the wicked armies. The last figure on the scene is Satan. For centuries he has oppressed people as "the god of this world" (2 Cor. 4:4 KJV) and "the prince of the power of the air" (Eph. 2:2 KJV). But the descent of Jesus to earth will mark the incarceration of the devil.

"Then I saw an angel coming down from heaven with the key to the bottomless pit and a heavy chain in his hand" (Rev. 20:1 NLT).

This isn't the first reference to the "bottomless pit" in John's revelation. Earlier, John described a fallen angel that was given a key to the abyss. He opened it, releasing all forms of demons (Rev. 9:1–11). On this occasion, the exact opposite will occur.

"[The angel] seized the dragon—that old serpent, who is the devil, Satan—and bound him in chains for a thousand years. The angel threw him into the bottomless pit, which he then shut and locked so Satan could not deceive the nations anymore until the thousand years were finished. Afterward he must be released for a little while" (Rev. 20:2–3 NLT).

I've seen pits. I've seen deep pits, caliche pits, garbage pits, even armpits. I've never, however, seen a bottomless pit. One awaits Lucifer. The fallen angel will become the falling angel, ever flailing and spinning but never landing.

After centuries of wreaking havoc; after two testaments worth of racism, misogyny, and conflict; after dispensing more pain, bloodshed, headaches, and heartache than words can describe, Satan will be out of the picture.

Imagine our world without him. No thoughts of despair. No moments of fear. No depression, deception, disease, or division. Satan will be sealed away for ten glorious centuries. He won't be cast into hell. Not yet, anyway. John cryptically informed us, "The angel threw him into the bottomless pit, which he then shut and locked so Satan could not deceive the nations anymore until the thousand years were finished. Afterward he must be released for a little while" (Rev. 20:3 NLT).

Why must Satan be released? Before providing an answer, John continued to describe what he saw. "Then I saw thrones, and the people sitting on them had been given the authority to judge" (Rev. 20:4 NLT).

This is us! Rescued. Raptured. Renewed. Rewarded. Wedded. And now, "given the authority to judge." Adam and Eve were given this power, but they abdicated their thrones. We, the descendants of Adam and Eve, will fulfill our role as coheirs with Christ in the kingdom.

We will be joined by tribulation believers. "I saw the souls of those who had been killed because they were faithful to the message of Jesus and the message from God. They had not worshiped the beast or his idol, and they had not received the mark of the beast on their foreheads or on their hands" (Rev. 20:4 NCV).

The tribulation, while terrible, will witness a revival so massive that the ingathering will be too great to number. These members of the heavenly resistance will either be martyrs or survivors. The survivors will enter the millennium in mortal bodies. The martyrs, those slain during Satan's war, will be resurrected and commissioned to govern with Christ.

As John described, "They reigned with Christ for a thousand years" (Rev. 20:4 NLT).

Make certain that two words are highlighted in bold and underlined twice: the words *with Christ.* Christ will rule on the earth. He will assume his throne. He will fulfill the covenant made to David. "Your house and your kingdom shall be established forever before you. Your throne shall be established forever" (2 Sam. 7:16 NKJV).

David's throne was in Jerusalem. So, Jesus' throne on earth will be in Jerusalem. The angel told Mary, "He will be great, and will be called the Son of the Highest; and the Lord God will give Him the throne of His father David" (Luke 1:32 NKJV).

Tally this up. Jesus will reign and rule on earth. We—the raptured, rewarded, and wed—will reign and rule with Christ. The tribulation saints will reign and rule with Christ.

But over whom will we rule? Who will our subjects be? Keep in mind that, though many people will die in the tribulation, many will survive it. These include the 144,000 Jewish evangelists and their converts. This remnant will repopulate God's earth in their mortal bodies. And we will govern them.

The three impediments to Utopia will be reversed.

Satan on the prowl? Not in the millennium. *Satan will be bound.*

Jesus is unwelcome in our day. But in the new era, *Christ will be enthroned.*

Unrighteous rulers currently exercise authority. In the millennium, *righteous rulers will govern.*

The result? Utopia. There will be no conflict. "Then wolves will live in peace with lambs, and leopards will lie down to rest with goats" (Isa. 11:6 NCV). Nature will be in harmony. Bears won't attack. Sharks won't bite.

Nations won't rage. "The LORD will mediate between nations and will settle international disputes. They will hammer their swords into plowshares and their spears into pruning hooks. Nation will no longer fight against nation, nor train for war anymore" (Isa. 2:4 NLT).

Those in mortal bodies will live long lives. "No longer will babies die when only a few days old. No longer will adults die before they have lived a full life. No longer will people be considered old at one hundred!" (Isa. 65:20 NLT).

This world, so upside down, will be right side up. People who were rejected in this life will be respected in the next. In this age they were enslaved and sold; in the next they will rule and reign. In this age they were handicapped and sick; in the next they will serve with perfected, glorified bodies. Billions have been victims of cruel tyrants; in the next age they themselves will rule with righteousness. In this life they were aborted and discarded, considered an inconvenience; in the next they will be rewarded and consulted. They will serve in the presence of Jesus.

The four covenants God made will be honored as promised:

- In Eden, God's children will rule over creation.
- To Abraham, Israel will have its soil.
- To David, his throne will have its king.
- To Jeremiah, his people will experience spiritual renewal.

This sounds like heaven. This sounds like the perfect ending. This sounds like the grand conclusion to the story of God. He has his garden. His perfect children reign with him on a perfect earth.

But then there is this surprise. Remember the parenthetical phrase about Satan? "Afterward he must be released for a little while" (Rev. 20:3 NLT).

John described what happens next.

> When the thousand years end, Satan will be let out of his prison. He will go out to deceive the nations of the world and gather them together, with Gog and Magog, for battle—a mighty host, numberless as sand

This world, so upside down, will be right side up. People who were rejected in this life will be respected in the next. In this age they were enslaved and sold; in the next they will rule and reign. In this age they were handicapped and sick; in the next they will serve with perfected, glorified bodies.

> along the shore. They will go up across the broad plain of the earth and surround God's people and the beloved city of Jerusalem on every side. But fire from God in heaven will flash down on the attacking armies and consume them. (vv. 7–9 TLB)

Satan, unchained for a short time, will recruit a force of rebels. Who would dare turn against King Jesus? "Gog and Magog" is a term for the enemies of God who live in remote regions (Ezek. 38–39). These will be those who are geographically separated from Jesus by distance and generationally separated from the tribulation by time. Far from Jesus. Far from their story.

Easy targets for Satan.

But war will never happen. John foresaw it: "Fire from heaven came down on the attacking armies and consumed them" (Rev. 20:9 NLT).

The battle will end before it begins. Satan will be thrown into the lake of fire. Gone forever. Tormented forever.

Tragically, he won't be alone. As John reveals the future, our next stop will be the most sobering event in history, the judgment of the wicked. But before we turn a page and ponder it, let's put a ribbon on this age and ask: What in the world can the millennium teach us?

Millennium Messages

My list consists of two thoughts.

We cannot underestimate the depravity of humanity. Not even a thousand years of peace and prosperity will cleanse the human heart of its selfish nature. Satan will find willing followers.

Who are they? And from where do they come? How can a perfect world tempt them?

During the millennium, two types of people will coexist: those with glorified bodies and those with mortal bodies. Glorified saints were either redeemed at the rapture or resurrected after the tribulation.

The rest of the population will consist of those saved during the tribulation. They will enter the millennium with mortal bodies. They will live long, wonderful lives and have children (Isa. 65:20). They will still have sinful natures. However, with Satan bound and the Lord Jesus himself personally present on the earth, they will not be tempted to sin. When Satan is released at the end of the millennium, his character will not be any different. He will go forth to "steal, kill, and destroy" (John 10:10 GNT).

Difficult as it might be to imagine, he won't be alone. Just as Adam and Eve sinned in a perfect Paradise, a throng of millennium dwellers will do the same. Satan will recruit an army so vast that "the number of them is like the sand of the seashore" (Rev. 20:8 NASB). They will stage a futile coup. Their actions will remove any doubt whatsoever about the sinful nature of humanity.

Even in the best of worlds, whether in Eden's garden or the golden millennium, Satan will seduce some people. We need a heaven-born righteousness. We need a Savior. When we enter our eternal state in heaven, we will do so knowing we are there by God's grace. We cannot underestimate our depravity.

Nor can we overestimate God's sovereignty.

God will accomplish what he set out to do. The earliest pages of the Bible declare God's intent:

> So God created human beings, making them to be like himself. He created them male and female, blessed them, and said, "Have many children, so that your descendants will live all over the earth and bring it under their control. I am putting you in charge of the fish, the birds, and all the wild animals." (Gen. 1:27–28 GNT)

God's plan from the get-go was a Paradise populated and overseen by his children. Our ancestors stumbled, but God's resolve never weakened. Adam and Eve turned from him, but he never turned from us. Paradise lost in Genesis is offset by Paradise found in Revelation.

What God says will happen, will happen.

Do we not need this reminder of God's control today? Do we not need the reassurance of God's steadfast hand on the steering wheel of humanity? Do we not need to be told and retold the story of God's plan and purpose?

The story of a boy named Beckham illustrates God's providence.

> Adam and Eve turned from God, but he never turned from us. Paradise lost in Genesis is offset by Paradise found in Revelation.

When Beckham was a toddler, he was found wandering the streets of Burundi looking for food. He was taken to an orphanage and soon adopted by a single parent who lived in the northwestern United States. Though the intentions of that parent were good, the demands of a child were too much for her. After a couple of years, she notified the adoption agency that she could not meet Beckham's needs. They needed to find a new family.

An alert known as a "second-chance adoption" went out to prospective families and agencies around the country. "A precious little boy in need of a family to provide a home and meet his needs." The news came to the attention of Maegan. She and her husband already had two children, but they were praying for a third.

They reached out to the agency. According to the law of the state, the prospective family was required to spend a week with little Beckham to test compatibility. Happy to oblige, the family traveled to the northwest, where they picked up the boy and drove to a beach house in Oregon. The week was glorious. The days were filled with laughter, games, and joy. On the last evening of the week, Thomas, the father, mentioned that the trip was coming to an end and everyone would be going home the next day.

Later that night when everyone was in bed, Maegan and Thomas heard Beckham crying in his room. They asked him what was wrong. He couldn't say. They asked him again. He still struggled to find the words. Finally he asked, "Was I good enough?" He told his parents-to-be that he had been informed the trip was a test. Only if he was good enough would he have a new home.

Thomas held Beckham close and assured him, "We chose you to be in our home before we ever knew you. We made a promise, and we will keep it."

Today Beckham is flourishing with his forever family.

Our Father has made an identical promise to his children. Before sin was in the heart of humanity, salvation was in the heart of God. God made a covenant. His promises are binding. His decision is fixed. He will have his garden. And we will enjoy it with him.

> Before sin was in the heart of humanity, salvation was in the heart of God.

In this world in which everything is upside down, isn't it great to know the world will be right side up?

The Utopia in Texas may not live up to the name. But the Utopia in God's plan? Just wait and see.

CHAPTER 14

Where the Soul Goes to Die

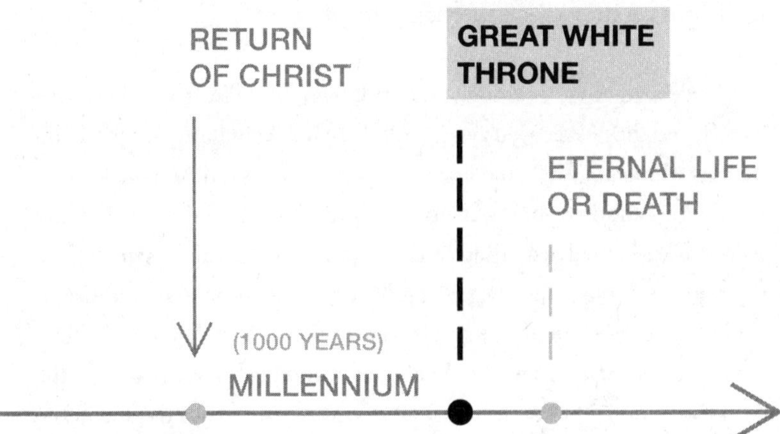

YOUR NAME APPEARS on some significant documents. Your birth certificate states where and to whom you were born. Your driver's license provides you an identification card to show the police officer when he pulls you over for speeding.

If you have a passport, it bears your name. A marriage license displays yours as one of two names. Social Security card. Diploma. Mortgage document. All of these contain a name.

Yet the importance of these pales in comparison to the one registry where your name needs to appear. The Bible teaches us about a book—the Book of Life. In the end this is the entry that matters. Driver's licenses will not be needed. Passports and Social Security cards will be relics from a distant day. But the Book of Life? The presence or absence of your name in it is, by far, the most important detail of your eternal destiny.

The book will be consulted in an event called the Great White Throne judgment. This occasion sits on the time line at the end of the millennium. Jesus will have overseen a world of peace, prosperity, and righteousness. Satan will be bound. Goodness will abound. At the end of the thousand years, Satan will finally receive his due: eternal agony in the lake of fire.

"The devil, who deceived them, was cast into the lake of fire and brimstone where the beast and the false prophet are. And they will be tormented day and night forever and ever" (Rev. 20:10 NKJV).

The fallen angel will fall one final time, never to be seen or heard from again. Good riddance, Lucifer.

This moment marks the end of earthly history as we know it. The millennial kingdom is finished. Our eternal state is next. But before the final age begins, a dramatic sentencing must occur.

> Then I saw a great white throne and Him who sat on it, from whose face the earth and the heaven fled away. And there was found no place for them. And I saw the dead, small and great, standing before God, and books were opened. And another book was opened, which is the Book of Life. And the dead were judged according to their works, by the things which were written in the books. The sea gave up the dead who were in it, and Death and Hades delivered up the dead who were in them. And they were judged, each one according to his works. Then Death and Hades were cast into the lake of fire. This is the second death. And anyone not found written in the Book of Life was cast into the lake of fire. (Rev. 20:11–15 NKJV)

One writer called this "the most serious, sobering, and tragic passage in the entire Bible."[1] It is easy to see why. It describes the final verdict in history and the darkest moment in time. John sees a:

- Great (formidable)
- White (pure)
- Throne (authoritative).

When John sees the throne, he also sees the end of this version of heaven and earth. "There was found no place for them" (Rev. 20:11 NKJV). The world as we know it will be no more.

Next, a courtroom scene. Jesus is seated on the throne. This is his rightful place. God has "given Him authority to execute judgment also, because He is the Son of Man" (John 5:27 NKJV).

Deeds Revealed

"Judgment day" is an unpopular term. We dislike the image of a great hour of reckoning. "Don't tell me what is right and wrong," we hear. Ironic. We disdain judgment but value justice, yet the second is impossible without the first. Heaven, our eternal home, will have justice. For that reason, the description of the judgment (Rev. 20) precedes John's portrait of our eternal home (Rev. 21).

Who is gathered before Jesus at the judgment? "I saw the dead, small and great, standing before God. . . . And the dead were judged. . . . The sea gave up the dead . . . and Death and Hades delivered up the dead who were in them" (Rev. 20:12–13 NKJV).

The dead are the unbelievers. We, the believers, will be raptured before the millennium. We will be alive and well. We will not be present at the judgment of the rebels. Is Christ your Savior? If so, then messages like this one are the closest you will ever get to the Great White Throne judgment. Only unbelievers will be present.

All the unrighteous humans who ever lived, from the beginning of time until the end of the millennium, will stand before the Great White Throne. This is their date with deity. They've avoided, denied, blasphemed, or mocked God. But now they have an appointment with him. Most of them died before the rapture. Some of them died during the tribulation. Others died during or at the end of the millennium when fire fell from heaven and consumed them.

They come from different eras. But they all come. God will call their bodies from the sea, the graves, the tombs. Their souls will be summoned from hades. They will gather unglorified before the throne, "small and great, standing before God" (Rev. 20:12 NKJV).

Small and great. Pauper and prince. Housekeeper and queen. Beggar and oligarch. Prisoner and tech billionaire. Status unimportant. Income level irrelevant. Diplomas vaporized. That which was dreamed of and schemed for will be dust and rust. MVP trophies, Pulitzer Prizes, PhD diplomas. Nowhere to be seen.

What remains are the books: "Books were opened. And another book was opened, which is the Book of Life. And the dead were judged according to their works, by the things which were written in the books" (Rev. 20:12 NKJV).

Two exhibits will be submitted: a set of books and a book. The set of books contain a detailed, meticulous account of the actions of every person. "God will bring every act to judgment, everything which is hidden, whether it is good or evil" (Eccl. 12:14 NASB).

The deeds of believers are recorded as well. The difference, the Everest-level difference, is that "there is now no condemnation for those who are in Christ Jesus" (Rom. 8:1). Jesus took our sinful deeds to the cross. When we said *yes* to him, Jesus "canceled the record of the charges against us and took it away by nailing it to the cross" (Col. 2:14 NLT). Jesus died for our deeds. Hence, our names are found in the Book of Life.

But what of those who never say *yes* to him? Or choose to deliberately say *no* to him? Their actions will be disclosed.

Could a more solemn, fearful thought be pondered?

"John Doe, your list of offenses is as follows. You judged your classmate as inferior because of her skin color. You deceived your teacher by copying another student's paper. You slugged your sister and denied that it was you. You lied about your homework. . . ."

Page after page will be read about adolescence alone! Dare we imagine the indictments of adulthood? "You misled your wife about the business trip. You flirted with your friend's husband. You cursed at your kids."

How utterly dreadful. There will be an arraignment but no advocate. Accusation but no refutation. Prosecution but no cross-examination. No investigation. No jury and no defense, just iniquities.

Their deeds will convict them. Even they won't defend themselves. Guilt will be obvious. It's just that simple. "Anyone not found written in the Book of Life was cast into the lake of fire" (Rev. 20:15 NKJV).

All the unrighteous humans who ever lived, from the beginning of time until the end of the millennium, will stand before the Great White Throne. This is their date with deity.

Destiny Determined

This verdict leads us to the most somber of biblical realities: hell. Scripture writers dip pens in the darkest inkwell to describe its nature. They speak of the "blackest darkness" (Jude v. 13), "everlasting destruction" (2 Thess. 1:9 KJV), "weeping and gnashing of teeth" (Matt. 8:12 NKJV).

It is a dreadful topic. Perhaps that is why people avoid the discussion of it. Have you noticed? We minimize it with our language. "That was a hell of a game." Odd that we don't use lesser tragedies as descriptors. That was a "cancer" of a baseball game. Or, that was a "famine" of a steak.

We sanitize it with our lofty opinions. *Any God who would allow for hell is not a God I would follow.* As if God must answer to us?

We weaponize hell in our sermons. "Turn or burn!" preachers declare in messages that feel high on shame, low on hope, and void of love.

Be assured, if a person takes hell lightly, he or she has not considered it deeply. And anyone who considers it deeply has grappled with this fair inquiry: "How could a God of love send people to hell?"

The problem with this question is the question itself. "People" implies neutrality and innocence. The hell-bound are not innocent. They are defectors. Hell is the chosen home of insurrectionists, the death row of insurgents. Hell is reserved not for those people who seek God yet struggle but for those who defy God and succeed in their rebellion. For those who say about Jesus: "We don't want this man to be our king" (Luke 19:14 GNT). So in history's highest expression of fairness, our just God honors their preference.

Should he do otherwise? Force his wishes on those who refuse him? Impose his plan on those who avoid him? By no means. Insurgents spend a lifetime ignoring his messages and mocking his name. People will stand before God who "didn't treat him like God, refusing to worship him. . . . They traded the glory of God who holds the whole world in his hands for cheap figurines you can buy at any roadside stand" (Rom. 1:21, 23 MSG).

Spend a life telling God to leave you alone, and in the end, he will do just that.

Be assured, if a person takes hell lightly, he or she has not considered it deeply.

God sends no one to hell. They volunteer.

They do so despite the repeated warnings of Jesus. Thirteen percent of his teachings refer to eternal judgment and hell.[2] Two-thirds of his parables relate to resurrection and judgment.[3] He wasn't cavalier or capricious, but he was direct. He often used the descriptor "outside." "Tie him hand and foot, and throw him outside, into the darkness" (Matt. 22:13). Outside of what? Heaven for certain. Outside the realm of redemption. Outside the court of appeals. Outside of all hope.

God sends no one to hell. They volunteer.

Abraham, in Paradise, told the rich man, in torment, "Between us and you there is a great gulf fixed, so that those who want to pass from here to you cannot, nor can those from there pass to us" (Luke 16:26 NKJV). Hell, then, is not a reform school where sinners are sanctified, not a purgatory where evil is purged. It is a "night on which no morning dawns."[4]

In a further expression of fairness, God matches the punishment with the crime. Just as there are degrees of reward in heaven, there are levels of suffering in hell.

"How much worse punishment, do you think, will be deserved by the one who has trampled underfoot the Son of God, and has profaned the blood of the covenant by which he was sanctified, and has outraged the Spirit of grace?" (Heb. 10:29 ESV).

Not all evildoers are equally evil. Some Jesus-rejectors are decent people. So decent, in fact, they assume their decency will save them. It won't.

Others make no attempt at virtue. They enslave people, molest children, ravage the innocent. They will experience appropriate pain. The punishment will fit the crime.[5] "And all were judged according to their deeds" (Rev. 20:13 NLT).

But what is hell like?

The historically orthodox definition is eternal conscious torment; exclusion from God forever and ever, left alone in darkness, "where their worm does not die and the fire is not quenched" (Mark 9:48 ESV).

A more depressing thought does not exist.

Others see hell as the place where the soul goes to die, not to suffer; a place of eternal punish*ment*, not eternal punish*ing*. An execution chamber instead of a torture chamber. Erase God from your life, and God will erase you from the next.

The language of certain scriptures lends credence to this interpretation.

"[The wicked] will be punished with eternal *destruction*, forever separated from the Lord and from his glorious power" (2 Thess. 1:9 NLT, emphasis mine).

"There is nothing but fear in waiting for the judgment and the terrible fire that will *destroy* all those who live against God" (Heb. 10:27 NCV, emphasis mine).

"For God so loved the world, that he gave his only Son, that whoever believes in him should not *perish* but have eternal life" (John 3:16 ESV, emphasis mine).

"Destruction." "Destroy." "Perish." Language of annihilation, perhaps? Satan and his minions will suffer forever. But insurgents? After proportionate suffering, might they be removed from existence? I deeply hope so.[6]

In the end, however, my opinion does not matter. Neither does yours. We might discuss the nature of hell, but only God defines it. It is against him that rebels have rebelled and sinners have sinned. Only he knows the number of invitations the hard-hearted have spurned, the slander they have spewed, and the pain they have purveyed. Only God knows the righteous verdict for the mutineer. Due justice will occur.

This much is clear: hell is horrible. This is a distressing, disturbing discussion. Sad for us and even sadder for God. Nothing in Scripture leads us to think God delights in the rendering of this verdict. Just the opposite. "I take no pleasure in the death of wicked people. I only want them to turn from their wicked ways so they can live" (Ezek. 33:11 NLT).

Did Jesus not yearn for the city of Jerusalem? When his people rejected him, he grieved, "Jerusalem, Jerusalem, the city that kills the prophets and stones God's messengers! How often I have wanted to gather your children together as a hen protects her chicks beneath her wings, but you wouldn't let me" (Matt. 23:37 NLT).

His heart was heavy on that day. His heart will be heavier on judgment day.

The Great White Throne. Such a cheerless, weighty event. What do we do with it?

The Choice Is Ours

The good news about this bad news is that it need not be your news. Christ has done everything possible to steer us in the direction of heaven. Remember the question, "How could a loving God send people to hell?" We can fairly ask it from another perspective. "How can a just God allow sinners in heaven?" The answer? Jesus Christ. He became flesh. He lived a perfect life. He died a sinner's death. He rose from the dead to validate his authority over life and death. What more could he do? He, in essence, places himself between us and the doorway of hell and says, "Over my dead body."

On December 12, 1984, a thick fog settled over a highway just south of London. At 6:15 a.m. a truck was involved in an accident. Within minutes cars were blindly plowing into the wreckage. Ten people were killed. Two police officers came upon the scene and began waving down cars. Many drivers ignored them and plunged into the fog. The police officers began to scream and shout; they even threw traffic cones at windshields, hoping to steer cars away from certain destruction.[7]

How much more has Jesus warned us? He has issued a thousand and one cautions. He has posted Do Not Enter signs on the highway that leads to hell. Those who enter eternal destruction do so with eyes closed and ears covered to his warnings.

Don't be among them.

Some years ago I decided to take Denalyn to a nice restaurant for an anniversary dinner. I selected a fancy, swanky, dress-up, get-ready-to-pay-for-overpriced-food restaurant. I called to make a reservation.

When a person has a restaurant reservation, their name is entered in the reservation book. It's written on the page. To have a table, my name needed to be in the book.

The reservationist did not have good news. "I'm sorry. We do not have an open spot on that date."

"You don't?"

"Not a one."

"What can I do?"

She paused and replied, "You can show up and hope."

The good news about this bad news is that it need not be your news.

"Show up and hope?"

"Yes, sir. Sometimes we have a last-minute cancellation. If you are in the waiting area when someone calls to cancel, I will get you."

"But there is no guarantee?"

"No."

"No certainty?"

"No."

"We could get all dressed up, yet be turned away?"

"That's likely what will happen."

Such a plan has no appeal to me. I cannot imagine telling Denalyn to dress up so we can sit in a waiting area and hope we get to eat.

I want a guaranteed place. I want a confirmed table. I want my name in the book.

And a billion times a billion times over, I want my name in God's book. Don't you want your name to be entered? For heaven's sake, don't just hope it is. Make certain it is. Christ has said yes to us. It simply falls to us to say yes to him.

CHAPTER 15

Finally, Home

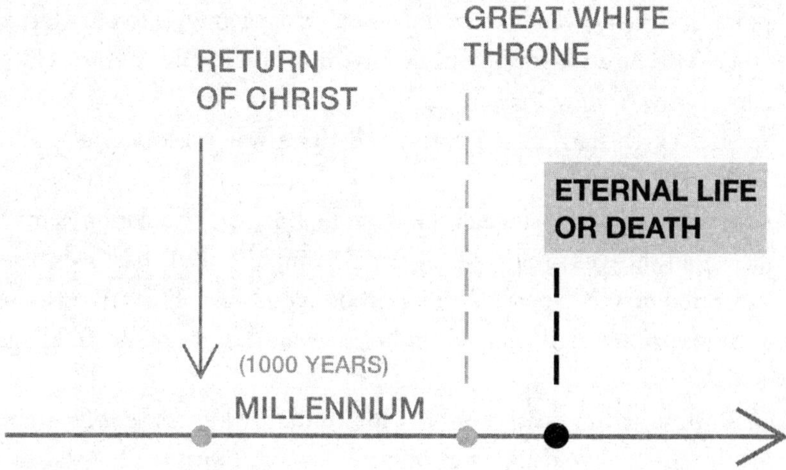

MY NIECE MICHELLE was adopted at the age of four months in 1969. She grew up in a loving, nurturing home. She and her husband, Jason, have raised two terrific daughters. They've led wonderful lives, and in 2023 she received a beautiful surprise. Michelle was contacted by her biological family. They had been attempting to locate her for years. Thanks to modern ancestral tracing technology, they found her.

Michelle traveled from Texas to Louisiana and Mississippi to meet them in person. She came to discover she has a half brother and sister on her mom's side of the family and three half sisters on her dad's side. Her father was unsure she existed. It was a grand gathering of stepsiblings, relatives, and friends. Meals were shared, stories were told, and introductions were made. Michelle sent pictures of the reunion to our entire family. In each photo she was beaming, and more than once she included this tender comment: "They said they've always been looking for me."

There is a lot of gospel in that comment. Your Bible, from the first page of Genesis to the final chapter of Revelation, tells that story. God is looking for you. He is searching, waiting, longing for the moment when the two of you will connect and never again separate. He has prepared a new life for you.

The word the Bible uses to describe that life is *heaven*.

As we saw in chapter 6, believers who pass away prior to the rapture will immediately enter God's presence in a place called Paradise. Yet Paradise is not heaven—not fully and completely. That's because Paradise is temporary, while heaven is eternal. Moving from Paradise to our eternal home, then, will be a transition unlike anything else in biblical history.

"Then I saw 'a new heaven and a new earth,' for the first heaven and the first earth had passed away, and there was no longer any sea" (Rev. 21:1).

As we reach this new stage on God's time line, the tribulation is over. The one-thousand-year reign of Christ is complete. Evil has been forever eradicated at the Great White Throne judgment. The villains and their minions are eternally cut off and cast away. The new and final age has come.

Our sin resulted in death not only for humanity but also for creation. "The earth will grow old like a garment" (Isa. 51:6 NKJV). The psalmist agreed: "You laid the foundations of the earth. . . . They shall perish . . . They will grow old like worn-out clothing, and you will change them like a man putting on a new shirt" (Ps. 102:25–26 TLB).

Our planet yearns for this masterful makeover. As Paul wrote:

> The creation waits in eager expectation for the children of God to be revealed. For the creation was subjected to frustration, not by its own choice, but by the will of the one who subjected it, in hope that the creation itself will be liberated from its bondage to decay and brought into the freedom and glory of the children of God. (Rom. 8:19–21)

The Greek language has two words that can be translated as "new." One is *neos*. It primarily refers to "new in time." If people say, "It's time for the new semester," they mean *neos*. The second word translated "new" is *kainos*. The term "denotes 'new,' or that which is unaccustomed or unused, not 'new' in time, recent, but 'new' as to form or quality."[1] In such a case the new is, as a rule, "different and superior in kind to the old."[2] This is the word John used in Revelation 21:1. The new earth will be a better version of the old, renewed to its intended splendor.

God reclaims his creation. He is a God of restoration, not destruction. Scripture is resplendent with "re" words: *re-newal*, *re-demption*, *re-gain*, *re-surrection*. God loves to *re-do* and *re-store*. Jesus used this language with his disciples: "In the re-creation of the world, when the Son of Man will rule gloriously, you who have followed me will also rule" (Matt. 19:28 MSG).

God will restore every atom, insect, animal, and galaxy to its original glory.

God will restore every atom, insect, animal, and galaxy to its original glory. To do any less would be the admission of defeat. To destroy the universe is to admit it cannot be reclaimed and renewed. To rescue and redeem it, however, is yet another display of our Maker's ultimate authority.

It will be time for a new start. John saw it coming.

The Holy City

"Then I, John, saw the holy city, New Jerusalem, coming down out of heaven from God, prepared as a bride adorned for her husband" (Rev. 21:2 NKJV).

This is the first time John speaks this way. The prior chapters contain more than twenty-five "I saw" statements. He saw "a white horse," "an angel standing," "the beast," "the kings of the earth," "an angel coming down," and more (19:11, 17, 19; 20:1; 6:15; see also 20:4, 11, 12; 21:1).

But when John sees the New Jerusalem, he does something different. He personalizes the moment. "I, John, saw the holy city, New Jerusalem" (Rev. 21:2). It's as if John can't believe he is the one to witness the metropolis. He's an archaeologist unearthing the Rosetta stone, a violinist playing the first Stradivarius. John beholds the crown jewel of heaven, the New Jerusalem.

He calls Jerusalem a "*holy* city."

"A holy city," explained one commentator, "will be one in which no lie will be uttered in one hundred million years, no evil word will ever be spoken, no shady business deal will ever be discussed, no unclean picture will ever be seen, no corruption of life will ever be manifest. It will be holy because everyone in it will be holy."[3]

How could Jerusalem be holy? "No longer will there be any curse" (Rev. 22:3). The curse is the consequence of sin, the hangover of rebellion. In the garden of Eden, Adam and Eve sinned. They expected a tree to give what only God could give: life.

To sin is to turn to anyone or anything for what only God can provide. To turn to a hard body or a Harvard degree for significance. To a bottle of Scotch or a night of sex for pain management. To religious busyness for guilt therapy. When we ask anything on earth to do heaven's job, we sin. And sin complicates life! It renders it as complex as a Rubik's Cube.

Calculate the time we spend undoing the damage of yesterday's sin. Fighting bad habits. Avoiding toxic relationships. Regretting poor choices. How much energy do you expend repairing yesterday's decisions? Life is complicated today because we sinned yesterday.

How much simpler would your life be if you never sinned? Never disobeyed God? Never ignored his teaching or rebelled against his will? Extract all the fights, binges, hangovers, addictions, arguments, lust, and regrets from your reality. Doesn't life grow awesome quickly?

Multiply your answer by a few billion and imagine how different our world would be if no one ever sinned.

No nation would war or starve. No tongue would gossip, no person would slander, no spouse would cheat. No bomb or temper would erupt. People wouldn't fear dictators or muggings. We wouldn't bury ourselves in debt buying what we don't need with money we don't have to impress people we don't know. We wouldn't beat ourselves up for stumbling yesterday, because in a sinless society we didn't sin yesterday and won't stumble tomorrow. Or ever.

Such is heaven. "No longer will there be any curse" (Rev. 22:3).

No more struggle with the earth. No more shame before God. No more tension between people. No more death. The removal of the curse will return God's people and universe to their intended state.

God Has Space for You

The New Jerusalem is being "prepared as a bride adorned for her husband" (Rev. 21:2 NKJV).

Want a glimpse of your new home? John can help us.

> The angel who talked to me held in his hand a gold measuring stick to measure the city, its gates, and its wall. When he measured it, he found it was a square, as wide as it was long. In fact, its length and width and height were each 1,400 miles. Then he measured the walls and found them to be 216 feet thick. (Rev. 21:15–17 NLT)

Behold the size of the New Jerusalem: fourteen hundred miles in length, width, and height. Large enough to contain the land mass from the Appalachians to the West Coast. Canada to Mexico. Forty times the size of England. Ten times the size of France and larger than India.

And that's just the ground floor. The city stands as tall as it is wide. Supposing God stacks the city in stories as an architect would a building, the New Jerusalem will have six hundred thousand floors. Ample space for billions of people.[4]

Ample space for you.

When did you discover the congestion of this world? Your father's schedule had no space for you. Your boss just couldn't find a space for you. The school had no space for you.

We learn early the finite nature of resources. There's not much space. Consequently, we get eliminated, cut, dropped, and refused.

And we grow cautious. Limited quantities make hoarders out of us. For fear of exhausting finances, we clutch our money. For fear of losing our job, we subvert our associate. For fear of losing land, we build a fence or go to war.

But with the dimensions of our soon-to-be home, God proclaims, "Enough space for all!"

"Then he showed me the river of the water of life . . . ; on either side

No more struggle with the earth. No more shame before God. No more tension between people. No more death. The removal of the curse will return God's people and universe to their intended state.

of the river, the tree of life with its twelve kinds of fruit, yielding its fruit each month" (Rev. 22:1–2 RSV).

Heaven's tree is so great it spans both sides of the river. Its harvest is so rich it requires twelve months to gather. An ample city with abundant provisions.

Is this not great news? Great news for the thousands who squeeze pennies out of dollars? Who make homes out of shacks? Who live not month to month but minute to minute? "Blessed are you poor," Jesus pledged, "for yours is the kingdom of God" (Luke 6:20 NKJV).

But dare we trust this promise? The answer is chiseled in the stone of the New Jerusalem.

God Has Grace for You

"She had a great and high wall with twelve gates, . . . and names written on them, which are the names of the twelve tribes of the children of Israel. . . . the wall of the city had twelve foundations, and on them were the names of the twelve apostles of the Lamb" (Rev. 21:12, 14 NKJV).

Who are these twelve sons of Israel whose names we read on the city gates? Simeon and Levi are listed among them. They were the two brothers who convinced a tribe of men to undergo circumcision and then, three days into their recovery, attacked and killed them all (Gen. 34). Judah, another of the twelve, mistook his daughter-in-law for a harlot, slept with her, and impregnated her (Gen. 38). Nine of the brothers conspired to kill younger brother Joseph and would have succeeded had Reuben not intervened. So they sold Joseph into Egyptian slavery (Gen. 37).

Warring, scheming hustlers and liars. Sounds more like the 2:00 a.m. nightclub crowd than it does a Hall of Fame of faith. Yet these are the names carved on the gate of the New Jerusalem.

Dare we mention the names on the foundations? Peter, the apostle who saved his skin instead of his Savior (Matt. 27:69–74). James and John, who asked for VIP seats in heaven (Matt. 20:20). Thomas, the dubious, who insisted on a personal audience with the resurrected Jesus (John 20:27–28). Their names make heaven's honor roll. These were the disciples who told the children to leave Jesus alone (Luke 18:15), who told Jesus to leave the hungry alone (Matt. 14:15), and who chose to leave Jesus to face his crucifixion alone. "Then all the disciples forsook Him and fled" (Matt. 26:56 NKJV). Matthew did. Peter did. Bartholomew did. Yet all their names appear on the foundations. Matthew's does. Peter's does. Bartholomew's does.

The names of the twelve tribes and apostles are unlikely material for heaven's engravings. But aren't we glad to know about them? We engrave monuments with the names of heroes and philanthropists, scholars and explorers. But what if we are none of those? What if our lives have been marred by addictions, anger, prison terms, or failures?

"I have grace for you," God says.

Not only is the Holy City spacious and gracious, but it is unimaginably beautiful. The foundations will be inlaid with "every kind" of jewel: jasper, sapphire, chalcedony, emerald, sardonyx, sardius, and on and on (Rev. 21:19–20 NASB).

The city itself will be crystal clear. Its surrounding wall will be transparent glass. In our world we build walls so as not to be seen. In the new world all will be guileless. No need to keep people at a distance. No secrecy, no need for security. Nothing hidden.

Each gate leading into the city will be hewn from one giant pearl. We tell jokes about the "pearly gates," but let's not miss their significance. John Phillips can help us:

> All other precious gems are metals or stones, but a pearl is a gem formed within the oyster—the only one formed by living flesh. The humble oyster receives an irritation or wound, and around the offending article that has penetrated or hurt it, the oyster builds a pearl. The pearl . . . is the answer of the oyster to that which injured it.[5]

The pearl is born out of pain.

So it is with the New Jerusalem. It will be born out of the pain of Jesus. Throughout eternity as you and I pass in and out of the Holy City, the pearly gates will remind us of our Savior, who took on the sin of the earth so we can experience the glory of heaven.

Speaking of our Savior, he will make the city splendid. The dimensions will be spectacular, and the materials will be stunning. The pearl in the gate, the gold in the streets—we've never seen anything like them. But it won't be the emeralds or structures that capture our hearts. It will be our

Throughout eternity as you and I pass in and out of the Holy City, the pearly gates will remind us of our Savior, who took on the sin of the earth so we can experience the glory of heaven.

Jesus. We will see him! We will touch the scarred hands, hear the calm voice. We will know him intimately. "The throne of God and of the Lamb will be in it, and His bond-servants will serve Him; they will see His face" (Rev. 22:3–4 NASB).

Pause and personalize that passage. Whisper to yourself (or shout it if you prefer), "I will see his face."

You will see God. You! You will see the One who has never not been, the One who has never given in, the One before whom all creation bows. You will see him. In your glorified body that will never fail, in a glorified city that will never decay, you will see the God of all glory.

In your glorified body that will never fail, in a glorified city that will never decay, you will see the God of all glory.

Can you imagine the moment in which "[God] will wipe every tear from their eyes, and there will be no more death or sorrow or crying or pain. All these things are gone forever" (Rev. 21:4 NLT)?

No more cemeteries, cancer, or crime. No more oppression, depression, or suicide. No more corruption, pollution, or disruption.

In my imagination I hear God, in his splendor, declaring over this weary world and her wounded inhabitants:

> Behold, I make all things new. I reclaim and redeem. I restore the years that the locusts and worms have eaten. I give anew the days that you have spent leaning on crutches and slumping in your wheelchair. I reissue the energy cancer took and the joy depression stole. The songs your deaf ears could not hear? The snow-covered alps your blind eyes could not see? The mysteries your feeble mind could not grasp? They are now yours to enjoy.
>
> Despots plundered your peace. The arm of justice fell short in your life. Hunger gnawed at your belly. Fear hounded your nights. Racism ruined your future. War ravaged your world. No more. No more tears. No more sorrow. No more death.
>
> I restore the good you wasted on the altar of folly, the hope you sold at the brothel of lust. And I bring to you Love—love you have pursued in forbidden arms, pathways, and ventures. The Love to which all other loves hint.

> Behold, I make all things new!

Can you imagine?

I can't either. But what joy is found in the attempt.

When I was a youngster, my dad took the family to Arlington, Texas, to visit the Six Flags Over Texas theme park. I cannot overstate my excitement. The highlight of my two-stoplight hometown was a groundhog park. Our idea of entertainment was an evening at Dairy Queen. Six Flags was everything our little town was not: colorful, musical, entertaining.

At one point while riding a trolley, I turned to my father and said, "This is the most wonderful place I have ever seen."

To which he responded, "That's great, Max. But we are still in the parking lot."

I had assumed the passenger shuttle was the big ride. I would have taken a tour of the entryway and called it a wonderful vacation. Good thing my father was there to tell me, "There is more on the other side."

That is God's message to you. He has a place for you, space for you, and grace for you. Lift your eyes and set your heart on your heavenly home. It's the one that will last.

God has a place for you, space for you, and grace for you. Lift your eyes and set your heart on your heavenly home. It's the one that will last.

AFTERWORD

Made for More

IN ONE OF HIS MOVIES, Jack Nicholson portrays a curmudgeonly New York City author who snaps at anything that moves. He is rich, lonely, bitter, and afraid. He has phobias like the Amazon River has piranhas, and they gnaw on him. He fears stepping on sidewalk cracks, using a bar of soap twice, and shaking hands with anyone. Every day he eats in the same restaurant, sits at the same table, and orders the same meal from the same server.

At one point his neurosis reaches a breaking point, and he goes to see his psychiatrist. He surveys the waiting room of patients and exhales a sigh. He avoids physical contact but can't avoid the impact of the sad collection of misery.

"What if this is as good as it gets?" he bemoans.[1]

Many people assume it is. They mistakenly think their fondest moment, deepest joy, and most profound experience happens sometime between birth and hearse. Someone needs to tell them the good news, "As good as it gets? In no way and by no means. If you are in Christ, this life is as bad as it gets."

Every page and promise of the Bible invites and excites with the lure of a new age and a renewed world. Your best life awaits you!

It only gets better. What's more, we have been handed an itinerary. We know what happens next. Let the promise of the next life define the way you spend this life. Live in the light of heaven.

Embrace the Brevity

Our days on earth are

- like "a shadow" (1 Chron. 29:15; Job 8:9 ESV).
- "like a breath" (Ps. 144:4 ESV).
- like "a mist that appears for a little while and then vanishes" (James 4:14).
- "like the flowers of the fields" (Ps. 37:20 NCV).
- "swifter than a weaver's shuttle" (Job 7:6 ESV).

During the celebration of my sixtieth birthday, I made one request. I asked my kids, all adult-aged, to indulge their dad in a teaching moment. Over the years they've grown accustomed to such exercises. Yet this one left them puzzled.

"I want you to depict my sixty years on this rope."

It was long and thick, the type a sailor might use to secure a boat. As they watched, I tied one end to a piece of furniture in our den. I walked the rest outside, where I threw it over the railing of our second-story balcony. It disappeared from view.

"Imagine that the rope continues forever," I requested as I handed each one a black marker. "Let the rope represent my eternal existence. In the context of my God-promised immortal life, indicate the duration of this earthly portion with a mark on this rope."

They began to smile and knowingly nod. Each one set out to make the smallest possible mark. One of them rightly said, "Dad, I can't make one small enough."

Our lives are that brief.

That's why we can pray, "Lord, help me to realize how brief my time

Let the promise of the next life define the way you spend this life. Live in the light of heaven.

on earth will be. Help me to know that I am here for but a moment more. My life is no longer than my hand! My whole lifetime is but a moment to you" (Ps. 39:4–5 TLB).

Embracing the brevity empowers us to endure the burdens. "Our light affliction, which is but for a moment, is working for us a far more exceeding and eternal weight of glory" (2 Cor. 4:17 NKJV). Since these days are fleeting, can we not endure them?

Think of it this way. Suppose I make you an offer: an all-expenses-paid, four-week vacation to the place of your choice. Five-star hotel? It's yours. Hike through the Alps? Grab your backpack. Tour the ancient ruins of Rome? Don your toga.

> Embracing the brevity empowers us to endure the burdens.

Your part, your only part, is this: you must endure a millisecond of discomfort. A pinch. A pinprick. A match flame on your skin.

Would you accept the offer?

Please know: I am not saying that your cancer, heartbreak, or depression is as painless as a pinprick. What I am saying is that in the light of eternity, it will last just a moment.

Can you endure just a moment?

Can you be strong for just a moment?

Can you hold on for just a moment?

If this life is a dot on an unending rope, does it not make sense to set your hope on the rest of the rope?

Anticipate the Beauty

"If then you were raised with Christ, seek those things which are above, where Christ is, sitting at the right hand of God. Set your mind on things above, not on things on the earth. For you died, and your life is hidden with Christ in God" (Col. 3:1–3 NKJV).

Paul's logic is clear. We have been "raised with Christ." We are "where Christ is." We are "citizens of heaven" (Phil. 1:27 NLT). He has "seated us with him in the heavenly realms" (Eph. 2:6 NLT). That longing we have for more? That dissatisfaction we feel? Those questions that we ask? Those are tugs from God pulling us toward him.

Imagine it this way. One night as you were sleeping, a string was tied around your big toe. You detected the tying of the knot but were too sleepy to respond to it. As you continued to slumber, someone started tugging the twine. Somewhere in your subconscious you felt a pull.

Still, you slept. You slept until your foot fell off the side of the bed and landed on the floor. It's a wonder you didn't do the same. You awoke with a start and looked down at the string. As you did, someone gave it such a yank that your foot popped forward as if your knee reflex had been tapped.

What would you do at this point? Ignore the pull and go back to sleep? Many people do. Someone from somewhere is drawing them out of their slumber, but they refuse to respond. They cover their head with a secular pillow and try to go back to sleep.

But then comes a super-yank. The death of a friend. The warning of a doctor. A birthday cake with too many candles. This pull is too hard to ignore. So you follow the string. It winds you down the hall, through the living room, and into the kitchen, where your family awaits you with a surprise birthday party.

God has tied a string on every person, not to the toe, but to the heart. He pulls. He pulls with the glory of a sunset or the pain of a chemo treatment. He seeks to awaken us. And every so often, he succeeds. Someone wakes up. Someone follows the string down the hall, through the rooms . . .

They do what Paul said: they "seek those things which are above, where Christ is, sitting at the right hand of God. Set your mind on things above" (Col. 3:1–2 NKJV).

Paul used two stout verbs here. The first, *seek,* means "coveting earnestly, striving after."[2] The idea is to seek heaven the way a sailor seeks the coast or a pilot seeks the landing strip.

If, perchance, we too quickly read the word *seek*, Paul also employed the verb *set.* "Set your mind on things above" (Col. 3:2 NKJV). This verb emerges from a Greek term that means "to set one's mind on, to be devoted to."[3]

I obeyed this passage in an earthly fashion. In 1988, we moved from Rio de Janeiro to San Antonio. Months before our departure, friends sent us a picture of a house that was for sale. It was a brick residence with a brown door and large front lawn. With one look, I was sold. I posted the photo in our kitchen and gave it multiple gazes a day. I studied its exterior and pondered its interior. I showed the photo to the girls and examined it with my wife. By the time we moved to San Antonio, I could have picked out that house from a dozen others. I was acquainted with my home before I reached it.

Christ wants you to do the same. He has changed your permanent residence. "Think only about the things in heaven" (Col. 3:2 NCV). "Keep your mind on things above" (GW). "Think about the things of heaven, not the things of earth" (NLT). "Pursue the things over which Christ presides" (MSG). These translations combine to declare in one verse: live in the light of heaven!

How heaven-minded are you?

- Are living and dying equally appealing options?
- As you dream about your future, do you dream beyond the grave?
- Do you ever look into the face of a fellow believer and think, *In a billion years, I'll still know you*?
- Are you to the point where a walk through the cemetery leaves you jealous?
- Do you plan more for your heavenly home than you do for the construction of an earthly one?
- Have you ever not bought something because it will have no value in heaven?
- Have you ever heard thunder and thought Christ was coming?
- Do you daydream about the moment you'll see your loved ones?

A day with no thought of heaven is a day poorly used. The soul needs hourly gazes into the life to come. You need to know what your departed loved ones are doing. We need to envision the rapture and the millennium. Let's imagine the New Jerusalem and the face of God. Heaven is the green vegetable on the spiritual diet. Be consumed with the things above.

One of my sermon-illustration books contains a story about a missionary and his little son. They moved from England to Central Africa in the company of four other adults. Three of them died. The health of the father began to fail, so he resolved to return to England. He and his boy bounced for days across Africa in an old, broken-down wagon. Upon reaching the coast, they embarked for England by sea. Within a few hours they encountered a brutal storm. The waves and wind combined to make the sound of cannon blasts and shake the ship from stem to stern. During a lull in the tempest, the father held and warmed his son.

A day with no thought of heaven is a day poorly used.

Presently the boy asked, "Father, when shall we have a home that will not shake?"[4]

I can't vouch for the story. The book provides no source. But I can most certainly vouch for the question. I've asked it. You've asked it. Each and every person has felt this world with its troubles and tremors and asked, "God, when shall we have a home that will not shake?"

His answer? "Soon, dear child. Very soon."

In C. S. Lewis's *Voyage of the Dawn Treader*, Reepicheep, the valiant mouse, resolves to discover Aslan's country. "While I can," he declares, "I sail east in the *Dawn Treader*. When she fails me, I paddle east in my coracle. When she sinks, I shall swim east with my four paws. And when I can swim no longer, if I have not reached Aslan's country, or shot over the world in some vast cataract, I shall sink with my nose to the sunrise."[5]

May God stir identical hunger in us. May we sail, paddle, swim, and, if need be, die with our noses to the sunrise, savoring the day we will be finally home.

In the ancient Scriptures a group of men known as the men of Issachar were applauded for understanding the times and determining how to live in them (1 Chron. 12:32). These are the twin convictions of a healthy Christian. So, aware of our Savior's imminent return, how should we live? How do we prepare? What should we do as we wait?

Citizens of sixteenth-century New England found the need to answer a similar question. On May 19, 1780, the morning sky became so dark that it seemed like night. Birds returned to their nests. Animals reacted in fear. Commerce ceased and panic grew among the people. More than one person wondered if the world had come to an end.

The Connecticut legislature was in session. The politicians saw the gathering dark and, like others, assumed something apocalyptic was taking place. One legislator made the motion to adjourn so the men could return home and get their houses in order for judgment. At that, Abraham Davenport rose to his feet. This sixty-five-year-old legislator from Stamford spoke against the adjournment.

> The day of judgment is either approaching or it is not. If it is not, there is no cause of an adjournment; if it is, I choose to be found doing my duty. I wish therefore that candles may be brought.

His reasoning prevailed. Candles were lit. The darkness passed. The mysterious eclipse was caused by smoke from Canadian forest fires floating into New England.[6] Jesus did not return that day. But he will return someday—someday soon.

In the meantime go about your life. Love your family. Do your work. Be kind to the poor and lend an ear to the confused. Share the gospel. Urge others to get ready and stay ready. Be like Mr. Davenport: "I choose to be found doing my duty."

"Since everything here today might well be gone tomorrow, do you see how essential it is to live a holy life? Daily expect the Day of God, eager for its arrival" (2 Peter 3:11–12 MSG).

We do not know when our Lord will come, but we know he will. May he find us watching.

Bonus Material from Max

The Olivet Discourse

The Olivet discourse is a sermon preached by Jesus three days prior to his crucifixion. It is recorded in Matthew 24–25, Mark 13, and Luke 21. This sermon is futuristic in nature and describes the seven-year tribulation that will occur before Christ returns. A common alternative view is to see the sermon as prophecy regarding the destruction of Jerusalem in AD 70. I see otherwise. For several reasons it seems clear that Jesus was addressing the last of the last days. Jesus described the generation of the prophecy. "I tell you the truth, this generation will not pass away until all these things take place" (Matt. 24:34 NET). The phrase "All these things . . ." includes not just the destruction of Jerusalem, but Christ's victorious return (24:29–31) and the judgment of "sheep and goats," those who helped Jesus' brethren and those who didn't (25:40). Since no generation has yet to experience "all these things," Jesus must be referring to a future generation. In addition, Jesus described the devastation that is to come. "There will be great tribulation, such as has not been since the beginning of the world until this time, no, nor ever shall be (24:21 NKJV). The destruction of Jerusalem in AD 70 was unspeakably horrific. Yet, it would not be described as a one-of-a-kind calamity. Jesus reserved that descriptor for an upcoming event: the great tribulation.

Daniel's Prophecy

Notable here is that the Essenes of the Dead Sea area (the ones who practiced strict rules of purity and holiness) were heavily influenced by the book of Daniel and other apocalyptic writings (especially Isaiah's) that predicted the end of the old age and the coming of God's kingdom. They expected the arrival of a messiah who would deliver them from oppression and restore Israel. We don't know if they had contact with the followers of Jesus, but their beliefs and practices were similar to those of early Christianity, and they had their "ear to the ground" already about this very prophecy.

The Temple Mount

The Temple Mount is the most disputed acreage on earth. At the time of this writing, it is overseen by the Muslim Dome of the Rock. Any suggestion of a third Jewish Temple seems unfathomable. Then again, for hundreds of years, any idea of a Jewish state was beyond comprehension. Yet, in May 1948, it was born. The who, how, and when of this reconstruction have not been disclosed to us. Scripture speaks of a third and a Millennial Temple. The third temple is prophesied by Jesus and by Paul as a place where the Antichrist will demand to be worshiped and commit sacrilege (Dan. 9:27; 11:36–45; Matt. 24:15; 2 Thess. 2:3–4). The Millennial Temple will be built by the Messiah (Zech. 6:12, 13) and redeemed Jews and Gentiles (Hag. 2:7; Zech. 6:15). The Temple Institute as well as the Temple Mount and Eretz Yisrael Faithful Movement are the two main Jewish organizations responsible for making preparations for the Third Temple.

More Reasons to Position the Rapture Before the Tribulation

- Revelation, chapters 4–18, the Bible's most detailed description of the tribulation, makes no mention of the church. The word *church* appears nineteen times in the first three chapters, but not once in the following fourteen. It is as if the church is absent from the tribulation.
- Jesus is described as the one "who delivers us from the wrath to come" (1 Thess. 1:10). Paul clearly stated: "For God has not destined us for wrath, but to obtain salvation through our Lord Jesus Christ" (1 Thess. 5:9 ESV).
- Revelation 19:14 depicts the church among the "armies of heaven" descending with Jesus for the Battle of Armageddon. The church can't return with Christ unless we have been taken into heaven with Christ.

Questions for Reflection

Prepared by Sam O'Neal

CHAPTER 1

Good to Go

Big Idea: We can face the problems of this life by focusing on the promises of the next. It's natural and healthy for us to be interested in what happens next because understanding the future empowers us to face the present.

1. With eternity in mind, what does it mean to be "good to go"?
2. Do you feel that you are "good to go"?
3. A key theme repeatedly surfacing in Scripture's teaching about the future is "it's all about hope."
    - Do you perceive a sense of hopelessness in today's world? In your community? Explain.
    - How does learning about God's plan for the future give you hope?
4. A second theme in Scripture's teaching about the future is "it's all about him," meaning Jesus.
    - Read 1 Corinthians 15:12–20. What can we learn about Jesus from this scripture?
    - What can we understand about the future from that passage?

5. What are some ways Jesus has produced hope in your life? (Think of three or more specific times when you needed hope.)
6. Read what Jesus had to say in Matthew 24:3–14 about the years leading up to the end times. What specific signs did Jesus say would precede his return?
7. Why was the reestablishment of the state of Israel in 1948 a significant event for biblical prophecy? For our future?
8. As followers of Jesus, what are some specific ways we can cry out "fourth quarter!" to those in our communities? In our culture?
9. Max describes biblical prophecy as the Serengeti Desert, with many on one side who feel intimidated and many on the other side who walk around with a big-game swagger. Where do you fall on that spectrum?
10. What are you hoping to learn or experience as you begin section 1 of this book?

Application: Take a moment to consider the main questions on your mind as you begin your study of *What Happens Next*. Which of those questions are you most interested in having answered? Write your questions in a journal dedicated to this book.

Lord Jesus, it is my sincere belief that I am good to go as a member of your eternal kingdom. As I read through the different chapters of this book, I ask that you please convict me of any ways I am not prepared for eternity, or of anything in my lifestyle or my way of thinking that needs to change considering your promises for the future. In Jesus' name, amen.

CHAPTER 2

It Looks Like Reign

Big Idea: God's plan in the garden of Eden was for humanity to have dominion over our world—to rule as his agents. That plan was put on pause because of sin, but it was not abandoned.

1. What new understanding did you receive in chapter 2?
2. As you read through the creation story, what caught your attention? What details relate most to your current phase of life?
3. Much of God's plan for the garden of Eden centered around the concept of dominion. In your own words, what did it mean that Adam and Eve were created to have dominion over animals, plants, land, and sea?
4. According to Max, God "temporarily suspended the garden-of-Eden plan. But he did not cancel it. He did not abandon it. He certainly did not abandon us."

- In what ways do you feel most keenly the reality of sin in our world?
- How have you seen or felt God's presence and support most clearly in the midst of our sinful world?

5. Read 1 Corinthians 15:45–49. What are some major similarities between Jesus and Adam? What are some of the main differences?
6. Max says, "The overarching message of the Bible is God's relentless pursuit of his family." Have you experienced God's pursuit of you? Explain.
7. What meant most to you about your first experiences with the gospel? How did you first encounter the truth that Jesus died to save you? Were there obstacles to overcome before you could accept that message?
8. Reflect on God's plan to redeem his original plan for Eden and what that means for your eternity.
9. Read Luke 22:29–30. What do those verses say about your own identity and purpose?
10. What obstacles make it difficult for you to say yes to everything God has offered you through Christ?

Application: Draw a line down the center of a page. On one side, write down your hopes and dreams for your future in this fallen world. On the other side, write down your hopes and dreams for your eternal future in God's perfected world.

> *Heavenly Father, I receive the truth that you have an eternal destiny planned for me. I accept the truth that all aspects of the future—including my future—are in your hands. And I say yes to my destiny of ruling and reigning with my Savior in the life to come. In Jesus' name, amen.*

CHAPTER 3

Compelling Covenants

Big Idea: As human beings, we are not floating in a void of uncertainty. Instead, all of creation is bracketed by several important covenants with God. No matter what else happens, God will keep his end of those promises. Have you considered that God's covenants include you? How does that affect your thinking about this life and the next?

1. How would you describe a covenant? What makes a covenant with God different from a covenant between people?
2. Max says, "What happens in the latter days will make more sense once you know what God promised in the early days. We can stand on the foundation stones of God's compelling covenants." Which of God's covenants or promises are foundational for your faith?
3. What promise did God make to humanity through his covenant with Adam and Eve?

4. God's covenant with Abraham was based on the twin promises of "seed" and "soil." How have those promises impacted the Jewish people throughout history?
5. Read 2 Samuel 7:12–16 to learn about the covenant God made with David—a covenant that pointed forward to the Messiah.
   - Which of the promises in those verses point to Jesus? Which promises are more specific to David's son Solomon?
   - Which of the promises in those verses have already been fulfilled? Which ones are yet to occur?
6. What promises did God make to the Jewish people through his covenant with Jeremiah?
7. Why are these covenants significant? How do these promises add to your understanding of God's plans for history? How do they add to your understanding of God's character?
8. How does understanding these promises broaden your grasp of what will happen next in history, including the end times?
9. Knowing that our heavenly Father has his hands on the wheel of history should help us feel peaceful about the future. What obstacles or uncertainties still cause you anxiety about what is to come?

Application: This week, initiate a conversation with someone about one or more of these covenants. Explain what you've learned about the way God's covenants not only color our understanding of the past but also shape our expectations of the future.

Heavenly Father, I affirm the truth that you always keep your promises. You have been faithful to me in the past, and I trust you with my future. Please reveal any areas of my life where I have allowed doubt, fear, or anxiety to creep in and cause separation between us. In Jesus' name, amen.

CHAPTER 4

God's Plan for the Ages

Big Idea: Daniel 9 is a critical chapter in the Old Testament because it gives us a reliable time line that covers most of human history. The accuracy of that time line boosts our confidence that biblical prophecy can be trusted for both the past and the future.

1. What surprised you as you read chapter 4? Explain.
2. Read the seventy-weeks prophecy in Daniel 9:20–27. What are your thoughts about this time line for biblical history?
3. What specific promises did God make to Daniel in those verses?
4. Much of Daniel's prophecy pointed forward to the Messiah. Where do you see specific connections with Jesus in Daniel 9:20–27?
5. Daniel's prophecy covers a total period of 490 years but is segmented into three blocks: 49 years, 434 years, and a final 7 years. How does Max explain the reasons for those different segments of time?

6. According to Max, "God stopped the 490-year countdown clock at year number 483. When the Jews rejected their Messiah, God pressed pause. There is a gap of time between years 483 and 484—a hiatus between the events described in Daniel 9:26 and 27." What is yet to happen during those final seven years?
7. What did you learn in this chapter about the future period of time often called the tribulation?
8. The pause in Daniel's prophetic time line allowed God to insert the church into history, which is why we are now living in the church age. What makes the existence of the church significant considering God's larger plans for humanity?
9. What reasons does Max include as to why we can trust biblical prophecy?
10. How has this chapter (and the rest of the book so far) helped you prepare for what will happen next?

Application: Write down any lingering questions you have about the time line laid out in Daniel 9 or anything you would like clarified more fully. Then take some time today to seek answers to those questions. Make note of the answers you find.

Lord Jesus, I believe, and I affirm, that you are the main protagonist in all biblical history and throughout all human history. You are the Messiah spoken of by Gabriel to Daniel, and you are David's descendant whose reign will never end. Please guide me over the coming days and weeks as I continue to learn about your plans, and please give me strength and confidence to face the future with faith. In your name, Lord Jesus, amen.

CHAPTER 5

Millenni-what?

Big Idea: Much debate surrounds the millennium as described in Revelation 20. There are many reasons to accept and hope for a literal golden age in which we will rule and reign with Christ.

1. Did this chapter give you new insights about the millennium? Explain.
2. When you read Revelation 20:1–6, what images and repeated phrases capture your attention?
3. Max identifies four ways of understanding the thousand years described in Revelation 20. How would you explain each of these approaches in your own words?
    - amillennialism
    - postmillennialism
    - premillennialism
    - panmillennialism
4. In your opinion, which of these approaches best aligns with Scripture? Why?

5. Max uses the acrostic P.O.W.E.R. to offer evidence for the premillennial position. Fill out that acrostic in your journal.

   P
   O
   W
   E
   R

6. Which of those evidences for the premillennial position do you find most compelling? Why?
7. What are some examples of biblical promises related to the millennium that have not yet been fulfilled?
8. What did you learn about Satan while reading this chapter?
9. Have your opinions and understanding of the end times changed over time? If so, in what ways have they developed or shifted?
10. Think back to the four pillars (or foundations) Max presents in section 1. Which pillar feels most significant to you when processing what is to come? Why?

Application: Look up the doctrinal statements on the website of your church or denomination to see if they include any statements on the millennium. If so, how do you respond to those statements? If not, consider contacting one of your pastors to see if your church has a specific position on the millennium.

Heavenly Father, I praise you for the authority you have demonstrated over history. You know the end from the beginning, and you are sovereign over both. Thank you for the promise of a future filled with peace, prosperity, and joy. In Jesus' name, amen.

CHAPTER 6

The People of Paradise

Big Idea: "Where do people go when they die?" It's a question that has haunted and intrigued us throughout history. Thankfully, it's a question that does have an answer. For followers of Jesus, there should be no fear of death.

1. When did you begin wondering about this question?
2. Before reading this chapter, how would you have answered the question "What happens to people after they die?"
3. Has your answer changed after reading this chapter? If so, how?
4. How would you explain the concept of Paradise to someone who has never heard of it? (How is Paradise different from heaven, for example?)
5. What are the three types of heaven referred to throughout Scripture?
6. Read Luke 23:39–43. What did Jesus say about Paradise while on

the cross? What do these verses reveal about the timing of when we will arrive in Paradise?

7. According to Max, our first business upon arriving in Paradise will be the healing of our souls. What might that healing look like or feel like for you?
8. Max says the saints currently in Paradise spend time praying for those of us still living here on earth. Are you encouraged by that idea? How?
9. Based on this chapter, what are you most excited to experience or enjoy in Paradise?

Application: The idea that saints in Paradise are interceding for and cheering for those of us here on earth is powerful. Write down the names of your loved ones who are currently experiencing Paradise. What might they be saying to you now if you could hear them? What might their prayers sound like when they pray for you?

Lord my God, as I think about the list of names I wrote down, I am so grateful that you are caring for my loved ones in Paradise. Thank you, Lord, so much. Thank you for the deep love you have shown to those I love, and thank you for the opportunity to continue loving each of these people for all eternity. In Jesus' name, amen.

CHAPTER 7

The Rebel and the Rescue

Big Idea: The rapture is the next stop on God's time line for history. On that day all who are children of God will be caught up with Christ to Paradise. The rest of the world will be left to deal with a monster known as the Antichrist.

1. What did you find most interesting or intriguing in this chapter? Explain.
2. How would you describe the Greek term *harpazo*, which is used in Scripture to describe the rapture?
3. According to Max, one of the promises in Scripture about our future is that a bad dude is coming: the Antichrist. Read Daniel 8:23–25. What can we say for certain about the Antichrist based on that passage?
4. Also read Revelation 13:1–10. How do these verses contribute to your understanding of the Antichrist and what he will do?

5. Max says that because of the rapture followers of Jesus will not experience the terrors of the Antichrist. "Christians, upon the signal of Christ, will be transported into the presence of Christ. This rescue could happen at any moment. It will be activated by the conclusion of 'the church age.'"
   - What are the main truths you understand about the rapture after reading this chapter?
   - How do you respond to the idea that the rapture could happen at any moment? What does that mean for your life?
6. Read 1 Thessalonians 4:16–18. What specific truths about the rapture are presented in these verses?
7. The rapture's impact will extend beyond Christians who are currently living. The bodies of believers who have died will also be "caught up" and transformed. What hopes do you have for a future heavenly body?
8. Based on your experiences and understanding of God, in what ways does the dramatic nature of the rapture reflect his nature and character?

Application: Take a few moments to examine your life during the past month—your routines, your work, your relationships, your finances, your habits, and so on. What are some areas you would prefer to change or adjust if you knew the rapture would take place tomorrow morning?

> *Lord Jesus, I affirm the truth that you are my Savior and you have a plan in place to save your people. I am so grateful to be included in that plan. I commit to being watchful and being ready as I simultaneously do the work you have called me to do and wait for the moment of your return. In your name, Lord Jesus, amen.*

CHAPTER 8

Crowned by Christ

Big Idea: After the rapture, our first moments in Paradise will be marked by a judgment—not to assign punishments, but to offer rewards for faithful service. We will be honored by Christ, and then we will give honor to Christ.

1. What did you enjoy most about this chapter? Explain.
2. Read 2 Corinthians 5:9–11. How do you feel as you anticipate this future moment of judgment we will encounter in Paradise?
3. How would you describe or explain the term *bēma*, which is translated "judgment seat" in the text? What did that term mean to Paul's original audience?
4. According to Max, "God loans each of us time, talent, and treasure. How we use them determines our recognition. Let's make it our aim to receive the crowns."

- What are some of the main resources or talents God has given you to use for his kingdom?
- What would it mean for you to use those resources in a way that warrants recognition and reward at the judgment seat of Christ?

5. One of the rewards we may receive is the crown of self-control (1 Cor. 9:25). What does it take on earth for us to receive that crown in heaven?
6. Another potential reward is the crown of influence (1 Thess. 2:19). How would you describe that crown?
7. Next is the crown of life (James 1:12). What is that crown, and how do we receive it?
8. Paul mentioned the crown of righteousness in 2 Timothy 4:7–8. What does it take to receive that crown in Paradise?
9. The final reward discussed in this chapter is the crown of glory (1 Peter 5:4). What is that crown, and how do we receive it?
10. The judgment seat of Christ will be a moment not only for receiving crowns but also for offering them. Whatever rewards we are given will be laid at Jesus' feet. Spend a moment picturing yourself at that scene. What do you see?

Application: Let's think practically and honestly about the five crowns mentioned in this chapter. Is your life currently proceeding in such a way that you are likely to receive those crowns? Apply your answer to each of the following.

The Crown of Self-Control
The Crown of Influence
The Crown of Life
The Crown of Righteousness
The Crown of Glory

Lord Jesus, I want to build a life that is worthy of you—one that contributes to your kingdom. I confess all the ways my actions and attitudes have fallen short of your standard so far, and I ask that your Spirit fill me, guide me, and convict me so that I may be worthy of recognition when I stand before you in Paradise. In your name, Lord Jesus, amen.

CHAPTER 9

A Marriage Made in Heaven

Big Idea: After the judgment seat of Christ comes another wonderful event in Paradise: the marriage supper of the Lamb. The church—meaning all who have been saved by Christ—will be joined with Jesus in a moment of continuing joy.

1. What questions came to mind as you read this chapter, or what information would you like to have clarified?
2. What does it mean when Scripture talks about the church as the bride of Christ?
3. When Scripture describes God's people as being part of the bride of Christ, how does that imagery make you feel?
4. Think about your own experiences with weddings. Where do you see connections between those events and our relationship with God?

5. Read John's description in Revelation 19:7–9 of the marriage supper between Christ (the Lamb) and his bride. What words describe that moment in our future?
6. Max writes about Jesus pursuing his bride. Looking back at your life, what are some of the ways Jesus has pursued your heart?
7. Max also says this about Jesus purchasing his bride: "In the first century, the groom was required to give money to the father of the bride. The measure of his love was seen in the price he was willing to pay. The measure of Jesus' love is seen in the same."
    - What price did Jesus pay for our salvation?
    - Why is it significant that Jesus was willing to pay that price for us?
8. What did you learn from this chapter about Jewish customs for engagements and weddings in Jesus' day?
9. How does that information add to your understanding of the church as the bride of Christ?
10. Being included in the bride of Christ is being set apart as holy. What does it mean to live in a way that is holy?

Application: Max suggests that you "let your wedding day define the way you live on this day." Take a few minutes to contemplate the connection between your current life and your future participation in the marriage feast of the Lamb. Write down any specific ways your betrothal to Christ can help you navigate the challenges and opportunities of your current life.

Heavenly Father, I say yes to every way you intend to prepare me for the marriage supper between Christ and his bride. I say yes to holiness and conviction. I say yes to faithfulness and truth. I say yes to living my life right now in a way that honors and pleases my Groom. In Jesus' name, amen.

CHAPTER 10

After the Saints Go Marching In

Big Idea: While the saints are celebrating in Paradise, the rest of humanity will have a much different experience on earth. The tribulation will be a season of chaos and destruction unlike anything ever witnessed.

1. For a moment, imagine the chaos and destruction of the tribulation. How would you describe that period of time?
2. What are some of the main methods God uses to catch our attention and lead us to himself?
3. Why do you think some people reject God?
4. Throughout this chapter, what did you learn about the seven-year period known as the tribulation?
5. Read 2 Thessalonians 2:9–10. How do these verses add to your understanding of who the Antichrist is and what he will do?
6. The book of Revelation offers a detailed and disturbing window

into what humanity will experience during the tribulation. As you skim through Revelation chapters 6–16, describe what happens during the following stages of that seven-year period:
  - The seven seals (chapter 6)
  - The seven trumpets (chapters 8–9, 11)
  - The two witnesses (chapter 11)
  - The two beasts (chapter 13)
  - The seven bowls (chapters 15–16)
7. Which of the judgments listed in those chapters feel most frightening to you? Why?
8. As you look around the world today, do you see hints of the chaos to come? Explain.
9. What can we learn about God's nature and character by studying the tribulation?
10. What are some good reasons for learning about the tribulation even if we are already saved?

Application: Spend a few minutes looking through news headlines from around the world. Where do you see events or themes that correspond with what you've learned about the tribulation?

Heavenly Father, I pray for every single person who will experience the terror of the tribulation. I ask for your mercy on humanity during those seven years, and I especially ask that you spare as many people as possible from enduring that crisis. Please pour out your Spirit on all nations and bring conviction in every way possible. In Jesus' name, amen.

CHAPTER 11

Now That the Chaos Has Come

Big Idea: Even during the depths of the tribulation, God will not abandon humanity. The reign of the Antichrist will be horrific, but God will redeem a huge harvest of souls.

1. What did you find most interesting or intriguing from this chapter? Explain.
2. Did you resonate with any particular moments in Jeff's story? If so, which ones?
3. To which parts of Emily's story did you relate? Why?
4. If the rapture were to take place tomorrow, how would it affect your community?
5. If you were Jeff's friend before the rapture and he told you his mantra "I need no Savior," how would you respond?
6. Describe your reaction to Pop's letter to Jeff.

7. Max says he would direct anyone left behind during the tribulation to Revelation 5. Take a few minutes to read that chapter.
    - What images do you find most powerful or noteworthy from that chapter? Explain.
    - How does that chapter add to your understanding of the person and work of Jesus?
8. Why is it important that Jesus has the authority to open the scrolls described in Revelation 5?
9. The ministry of 144,000 Jewish evangelists and the two witnesses described in Revelation 11 will lead to an unprecedented number of people saved during the tribulation. What factors might lead people to embrace the gospel during those years?
10. As followers of Jesus in the present day, what opportunities do we have to help prepare others for the rapture and the tribulation?

Application: Make a list of your friends and family members who, to the best of your knowledge, may not be saved. Commit to praying for five people on that list every day for a week.

Heavenly Father, I am so grateful that even during the tribulation, you will be active in saving souls. It is my desire to be similarly active now. For that reason, Holy Spirit, please give me the eyes to see and recognize those in my circle of friends and family members who may not be members of your kingdom. Please give me the words to say that will help lead to conviction and salvation. Please use me as a messenger of your grace and truth. In Jesus' name, amen.

CHAPTER 12

The Crowns and the Crimson

Big Idea: Jesus' first incarnation was as the Lamb of God who takes away the sin of the world. His next incarnation will be as the King of kings who judges the sin of the world.

1. What questions came to mind as you read through this chapter?
2. What words would you use to describe Jesus' nature and character?
3. According to Max, the return of Jesus "is the central focus of prophecy and a dominating theme of all Scripture." In your opinion, why will Jesus' return be such a significant event in the scope of history?
4. Read Matthew 24:29–31 to see what Jesus himself said about his second coming.
   - What ideas or images catch your attention when you read those verses? Explain.

- What are some possible reasons why the people of earth will mourn when they see evidence in the sky of Jesus' return?

5. What is the significance of Jesus wearing many crowns at his return?
6. Max writes, "White horse. Countless crowns. Blazing eyes. Bloody robe. This is not your baby Jesus, meek and mild. This is your King Jesus, mighty and riled." How do these descriptions fit with your understanding of Jesus' character? His mission and purpose?
7. When Jesus returns, he will demonstrate judgment and condemnation upon all who rebelled against his kingdom. By that point in history, what opportunities will those rebels have had to recognize the error of their ways and repent?
8. Why is it necessary for Jesus to deliver judgment and condemnation as the true King of this world?
9. What gives you confidence that Jesus will fulfill his promise to return to our world and judge God's enemies?
10. How should we understand the biblical truth that every knee will bow and every tongue confess the lordship of Jesus? (Phil. 2:10–11). What does that mean on a practical level?

Application: If possible in your current space, use your physical posture to express your worship of Jesus by kneeling. Take a knee in submission to your Savior, and then confess with your mouth that he is Lord. Declare him to be Lord over every area of your life—especially those areas in which you have difficulty submitting to him.

Lord Jesus, I declare in this moment that you are already King. You are King of the universe and King of our world—the King of kings. You are my King, and I bow my knee in submission to you. I confess with my tongue that you are Lord and there is no other. May your will be done both now and at the end of this age. In your name, Lord Jesus, amen.

CHAPTER 13

God Will Have His Garden

Big Idea: The millennium is a concept that sometimes causes confusion and debate for Bible students, but the overall message of Scripture points to a future thousand-year period of peace, prosperity, and joy on earth.

1. What did you enjoy most from this chapter? Explain.
2. Do you see evidence that people in today's culture are longing for a better world? A more perfect world? If so, describe the evidence.
3. Max offers three reasons Utopia is not possible in our current world. Take a moment to explain each of these reasons.
   - Satan is on the loose.
   - Jesus is unwelcome.
   - Our rulers are unrighteous.
4. What are some ways you have experienced each of those realities

in your own life? (What evidence have you encountered for the truth of each of those three statements?)

5. Read Revelation 20:1–6. What did the apostle John's vision reveal about the millennium? What ideas or images stand out to you from those verses? Explain.
6. During the millennium, Satan will be removed from our world for a thousand years. How could that reality alone change our world?
7. Not only will Satan be removed, but Jesus will take his rightful place as Lord and King. What changes will that make in our world and our experiences?
8. How will the millennium fulfill the four promises mentioned back in chapter 3 of this study guide?
    - God's covenant with Adam and Eve
    - God's covenant with Abraham
    - God's covenant with David
    - God's covenant with Jeremiah
9. What are some possible reasons that God would release Satan at the end of the millennium? What purposes might that serve?
10. How does the future reality of the millennium impact your life in the present?

Application: The promise of the millennium is a thousand years of peace and prosperity, not floating on an ethereal cloud but experiencing life right here on earth. Write down what you want your life to look like during that period. Be specific.

Heavenly Father, I lift up my voice to declare my desire for a world in which Satan no longer has any influence or power. I desire a world in which Jesus is welcome and recognized as King. And I desire a world in which every ruler is a righteous extension of your will and your character. Please, Father, bring that world here in your timing! In Jesus' name, amen.

CHAPTER 14

Where the Soul Goes to Die

Big Idea: Hell is real, and hell will be the real experience of all who reject Christ. But for those whose names are written in the Book of Life, we need have no fear of eternity.

1. What thoughts were stirred as you read through this chapter?
2. Read about the Great White Throne judgment in Revelation 20:11–15.
    - How would you describe this moment? What will happen?
    - What is the second death described in this passage?
3. Why is it necessary for God to function as the judge of all people?
4. How would you describe or explain the two sets of books that will be presented during the Great White Throne judgment?
5. As a child, what were you taught about hell?

6. How have your beliefs on the topic of hell changed or shifted over the years?
7. Describe some of the ideas people in our culture have about hell.
8. Max addresses a common question in today's world: "How could a loving God send people to hell?" How would you answer that question?
9. In your own words, summarize the following two conceptions of hell mentioned in this chapter:
    - eternal conscious torment
    - annihilationism (or destruction)
10. What does it take for someone to have their name written in the Book of Life?

Application: Once again, take several minutes today (and even throughout the day) to pray for any of your friends and family members who may be on a spiritual trajectory that will lead to hell. To separation from God. Lift up those individuals to God, praying for the conviction of sin and a call toward righteousness.

> *Lord Jesus, please have mercy on us! Lord Jesus, please have mercy on all whose names are not written in the Book of Life. Please send your Spirit to bring the dead to life, to help us feel conviction, and to move us to confession of our sin. Please ignite a revival in my community, and please show me anything and everything I can do to be a worker for your kingdom. In your name, Lord Jesus, amen.*

CHAPTER 15

Finally, Home

Big Idea: For all whose names are written in the Book of Life, God is even now preparing us an eternal home. This is the future place we call heaven, and it is the place where we will see God face-to-face.

1. Take a few moments to picture heaven and the home God is preparing for you. Describe it.
2. In what specific ways have you responded to God's pursuit of you?
3. What is the difference between Paradise and heaven?
4. Read Romans 8:19–21. What do those verses mean for what we currently know as creation? What will happen to our world after the millennium?
5. Read Revelation 21:9–21 and note John's description of the New Jerusalem, which is another term for heaven.
   - What ideas or images catch your attention?
   - Based on these verses, what are some words you would use to describe our eternal home?

6. Read Revelation 22:1–5. How do those verses add to your understanding of what heaven will be like?
7. According to Max, "God has space for you." What did you learn in this chapter about the size of the New Jerusalem?
8. God also has grace for you. Why are the names engraved on the gates and foundations of the New Jerusalem significant?
9. Think about the moment you see God face-to-face. What emotions do you experience when you contemplate that meeting?

Application: Take a moment to contemplate your current home. What do you like best about that space? What do you like best about your neighborhood? Your living situation? Now project forward to your eternal home. What are you looking forward to most about your life in the New Jerusalem?

Lord Jesus, I believe the words of Scripture that you are preparing a place for me even now. I believe you are preparing a home for all who follow you. I am so grateful! Thank you, Lord, for your goodness toward me. Thank you, Lord, for your provision both now and in the future. Thank you, Lord, for all you have done and all you have promised to do. In your name, Lord Jesus, amen.

CHAPTER 16

Made for More

Big Idea: What we have experienced so far is only the very beginning of the very beginning of all God has prepared for us in eternity.

1. What did you find most interesting or significant in this final chapter? Explain.
2. Scripture often speaks of human life as brief—like a shadow, a mist, or a breath. How have you experienced the brevity of life?
3. Why is it important for us to embrace this life's brevity?
4. Max describes the startling moments of our lives as God's tugs on the toe, attempting to wake us from sleep. What were some of the tugs that helped you wake up?
5. In your experience, what are some of the main reasons people choose to stay spiritually asleep?
6. Read Colossians 3:1–3 and note what Paul wrote about living with eternity in mind.
    - What are the benefits of setting our minds "on things above," where Christ is?

- What makes it challenging for us to keep that perspective?

7. According to Max, "A day with no thought of heaven is a day poorly used. The soul needs hourly gazes into the life to come." What are some specific ways we can anticipate the beauty and joy of our heavenly home?
8. What are some specific ways we can live each day looking forward to the return of Jesus?
9. What have you found most interesting or helpful to your spirit during your study of this book?
10. What questions would you still like to have answered or explained after reading the final chapter? Where can you go for more information?

Application: Write down several of your most joyful moments—those moments when you experienced the greatest heights of happiness, amazement, and wonder. Once you have a list, identify what those moments from your short, temporary life on this earth can teach you about what's in store for you in heaven.

Heavenly Father, I am grateful for the opportunity to study your Word and contemplate what happens next in history. I am grateful for the ability to think deeply about the rapture, the tribulation, the marriage supper of the Lamb, the millennium, and the New Jerusalem. Thank you, Father, for caring enough about your people to show us what happens next so that we can face the future with faith. In Jesus' name, amen.

Notes

Chapter 1: Good to Go

1. John MacArthur, *The MacArthur New Testament Commentary:* Revelation 12–22 (Chicago: Moody Publishers, 2000), 262.
2. Mark Hitchcock, *The End: Everything You'll Want to Know about the Apocalypse* (Carol Stream, Il. Tyndale, 2018),4–5.
3. Ellyn Maese, "Almost a Quarter of the World Feels Lonely," *Gallup* (blog), October 24, 2023, news.gallup.com/opinion/gallup/512618/almost-quarter-world-feels-lonely.aspx.
4. "Any Anxiety Disorder," NIH National Institute of Mental Health, https://www.nimh.nih.gov/health/statistics/any-anxiety-disorder.
5. "Suicide," National Institute of Mental Health (NIMH), https://www.nimh.nih.gov/health/statistics/suicide.
6. "Alcohol and Drug Abuse Among Young Adults," American Addiction Centers, updated April 4, 2024, https://americanaddictioncenters.org/addiction-statistics/young-adults#.
7. "Latest Federal Data Show That Young People Are More Likely Than Older Adults to Be Experiencing Symptoms of Anxiety or Depression," March 20, 2023, KFF, https://www.kff.org/mental-health/press-release/latest-federal-data-show-that-young-people-are-more-likely-than-older-adults-to-be-experiencing-symptoms-of-anxiety-or-depression.
8. Adam Piore, "Scientists' Understanding of Anxiety is Radically Evolving—But How Long Will It Take for Treatments to Catch Up?" *Newsweek*,

September 5, 2019, https://www.newsweek.com/2019/09/20/anxiety-medication-drugs-science-exercise-brain-1457006.html.

9. Deidre McPhillips, "Suicide Deaths Reached a Record High in the US in 2022, Despite Hopeful Decreases Among Children and Young Adults," CNN, November 29, 2023, https://www.cnn.com/2023/11/29/health/suicide-record-high-2022-cdc?cid=ios_app.
10. C. S. Lewis, *Mere Christianity* (New York: MacMillan, 1960), 104.
11. Gayle Spinazze, "Press Release: Doomsday Clock Set at 90 Seconds to Midnight," January 24, 2023, *Bulletin of the Atomic Scientists*, https://thebulletin.org/2023/01/press-release-doomsday-clock-set-at-90-seconds-to-midnight/.
12. Jeff Diamant, Pew Research Center, "About Four-in-Ten U.S. Adults Believe Humanity is 'Living in the End Times,'" Pew Research Center, December 8, 2022, https://www.pewresearch.org/short-reads/2022/12/08/about-four-in-ten-u-s-adults-believe-humanity-is-living-in-the-end-times/.
13. Atlas, Dr. J. Frank Norris, "Letter on Israel to President Harry S. Truman," Bible Forum Archives, AV1611.com, September 20, 2008, https://av1611.com/forums/showthread.php?t=498.
14. David McCullough, *Truman* (New York: Simon & Schuster, 1992), 617–620.
15. See also Isa. 43:5–6, 60:8–10, 61:4–6; Jer. 16:14–16, 23:3; Ezek. 11:17–20; 37:1–28.
16. John Gilmore, *Probing Heaven, Key Questions on the Hereafter* (Grand Rapids, MI: Baker Book House, 1989), 65.

Part 1: Four Big Ideas

1. Francesca Street, "What Happened on the Qantas Flight to Nowhere," CNN, updated October 12, 2020, https://www.cnn.com/travel/article/qantas-flight-to-nowhere-passenger-experience/index.html.

Chapter 2: It Looks Like Reign

1. Diana Durán, Ana Vanessa Herrero, and Terrence McCoy, "How Four Children Survived Amazon Place Crash, 40 Days Alone in Jungle," *Washington Post*, June 17, 2023, https://www.washingtonpost.com/world/2023/06/17/children-plane-crash-survivors-amazon-colombia/.
2. Do you say yes to Christ? I'm thrilled for you! I'll see you in Paradise! In the meantime, take the first steps of faith. Find a church where you can be baptized, learn about the Bible, and belong to a family of faith.

Chapter 3: Compelling Covenants

1. Additional covenants are the Noahic Covenant (Gen. 9:1–17; cf. 1 Peter 3:18–22; 2 Peter 2:5) and the Mosaic, or Old Covenant (Ex. 19–24, Deut. 11).

2. Michael Vlach, *Premillennialism* (Los Angeles: Theological Studies Press, 2015), 19.
3. Jeremiah, *The Book of Signs*, 7.
4. Mark Hitchcock, *The End: Everything You'll Want to Know About the Apocalypse* (Carol Stream, IL: Tyndale Momentum, 2018), 85.
5. Charles Swindoll, *Swindoll's Living Insights New Testament Commentary* (Wheaton, IL: Tyndale House, 2014), 123.
6. Wikipedia, s.v. "aliyah," last modified May 3, 2024, https://en.wikipedia.org/wiki/Aliyah.
7. Lidar Gravé-Lazi (Gravé-Lazi), "Israel's Population to Reach 20 Million By 2065," *Jerusalem Post*, updated May 22, 2017, https://www.jpost.com/israel-news/report-israels-population-to-reach-20-million-by-2065-492429.

Chapter 4: God's Plan for the Ages

1. Sir Robert Anderson, *The Coming Prince* (Grand Rapids, MI: Kregal, 1954), 122, 128*; Renald Showers, The Most High God: A Commentary on the Book of Daniel* (Westville, NJ: The Friends of Israel Gospel Ministry, 1982); John F. Walvoord, *Daniel—The John Walvoord Prophecy Commentaries*, revised and edited by Charles Dyer and Phillip Rawley (Chicago: Moody Publishers, 2012), 279.
2. Harold W. Hoehner, *Chronological Aspects of the Life of Christ* (Grand Rapids, MI: Zondervan, 1977), 47–65, 131.
3. David Jeremiah, *The Handwriting on the Wall—Secrets from the Prophecy of Daniel* (Nashville, TN: Thomas Nelson), 195.
4. Tyler Perry, "The Siege of Jerusalem in 70 CE," *World History Encyclopedia*, May 2, 2022, https://www.worldhistory.org/article/1993/the-siege-of-jerusalem-in-70-ce/.
5. "Our Story," Chosen People Ministries, https://www.chosenpeople.com/our-mission/our-story/; Jeremiah, *Handwriting on the Wall*, 185.
6. Isaac Newton, *Observations Upon the Prophecies of Daniel and the Apocalypse of St. John* (Cambridge, UK: J. Darby and T. Browne, 1733), see chapter 10, "Of the Prophecy of the Seventy Weeks."
7. Bill Creasy, Daniel, 2nd ed. (recorded lectures), (UCLA: Logos Bible Study, 2014), Audible, 4.58.00, https://www.audible.com/pd/Daniel-Audiobook/B005FR6M8C.
8. Hitchcock, *The End*, 68

Chapter 5: Millenni-what?

1. Jeremiah, *The Book of Signs*, 364.
2. A helpful tool on the differences of these opinions is George Eldon Ladd's *The Meaning of the Millennium: Four Views* (Downers Grove, IL: InterVarsity, 1978).

3. Other passages that seem best described by a one-thousand-year reign include Psalm 72:8–14 and Zechariah 14:5–17.
4. Hitchcock, *The End*, 412. Philip Schaff, *History of the Christian Church*, vol. II (Grand Rapids, MI: Eerdmans, 1910, rep. 1995), 614. "The most striking point in the eschatology of the ante-Nicene age is the prominent chiliasm, or millenarianism, that is the belief of a visible reign of Christ in glory on earth with the risen saints for a thousand years, before the general resurrection and judgment."
5. Papias as quoted in Eusebius Ecclesiastical History Vol. 1 (Cambridge, MA: Harvard University Press, 1926), 297. Thomas D. Ice, "A Brief History of Early Premillennialism," May 2009, chrome-extension://efaidnbmnnnibpcajpcglclefindmkaj/https://digitalcommons.liberty.edu/cgi/viewcontent.cgi?article=1021&context=pretrib_arch.
6. Justin Martyr, "The Dialogue with Trypho" (chapter LXXX, para. 239), in *Ante-Nicene Fathers: The Writings of the Fathers down to A.D. 325, Vol. 1: The Apostolic Fathers, Justin Martyr, Irenaeus,* eds. Alexander Roberts and James Donaldson. Revised and chronologically arranged with brief prefaces and occasional notes by A. Cleveland Coxe (New York: Christian Literature Publishing, 1885), CCEL.org, https://ccel.org/ccel/justin_martyr/dialog_with_trypho/anf01.viii.iv.lxxx.html.
7. Rev. 13:16–18.

Part 2: What's Next and Why It Matters

1. Rev. 1:8, 4:8, 11:17, 15:3, 16:7, 16:14, 19:15, 21:22.

Chapter 6: The People of Paradise

1. Rick Reilly, "Chillin' with the Splinter," *Sports Illustrated*, June 30, 2003, https://vault.si.com/vault/2003/06/30/chillin-with-the-splinter.
2. Epicurus, "Letter to Menoeceus" in *Letters, Principal Doctrines and Vatican Sayings* trans. Russell M. Geer (London, UK: Pearson, 1964).
3. Quoted in John Blanchard, *Whatever Happened to Hell?* (Wheaton, IL: Crossway Books, 1995), 62.
4. Robert G. Ingersoll, "A Tribute to Ebon C. Ingersoll," *The Works of Robert G. Ingersoll in Twelve Volumes* (New York: Dresden Publishing Co., 1912), quoted in Billy Graham, *Peace with God: The Secret of Happiness* (Nashville, TN: Thomas Nelson, 2017), 102.
5. Harald Lindstrom, *Wesley and Sanctification* (Willmore, KY: Francis Asbury, 1980), 121.
6. Randy Alcorn, *Heaven: A Comprehensive Guide to Everything the Bible Says About Our Eternal Home* (Wheaton, IL: Tyndale Momentum, 2004), 55–56.
7. Anthony Hoekema, *The Bible and the Future* (Grand Rapids, MI: Eerdmans, 1979), 104.

8. "Let's Go: Yosemite in Two Days," Yosemite.com, https://www.yosemite.com/itineraries/yosemite-in-two-days/.
9. Quoted in Henry Barclay Swete, *The Holy Catholic Church: The Communion of the Saints* (London: Macmillan, 1915), 222; Bloesch, 155.
10. Charles Wesley, author, "Come, Let Us Join Our Friends Above" (1759), *The United Methodist Hymnal* (Plainfield, IN: The United Methodist Publishing House, 1989), 709.
11. Calvin Miller, *The Divine Symphony* (Minneapolis, MN: Bethany, 2000), 139.
12. Linda Davis, "Where Will They Find My Boots?" #BecauseFiction Magazine November 2021, https://www.becausefiction.com/november-2021-historical-issue.

Chapter 7: The Rebel and the Rescue

1. James Strong, *Strong's Expanded Exhaustive Concordance of the Bible* (Nashville, TN: Thomas Nelson, 2009), s.v. "harpazō."
2. Hitchcock, *The End*, 253.
3. Strong, *Strong's Concordance*, s.v. "ḥîḏâ."
4. Dwight J. Pentecost, *Things to Come: A Study in Biblical Eschatology* (Grand Rapids, MI: Zondervan, 1964), 235.
5. *Strong's*, s.v. "keleusma," "From Aeschylus and Herodotus down, an order, command, specifically, a stimulating cry, either that by which animals are roused and urged on by man, as horses by charioteers, hounds by hunters, etc., or that by which a signal is given to men, e.g. to rowers by the master of a ship . . . to soldiers by a commander (Thucydides 2, 92)," in BLB Lexicon Resources—Thayer's Greek Lexicon.
6. Quoted in David Jeremiah, *Turning Point*, "At Any Moment (Pt. 2): The Great Disappearance," October 4, 2023, https://www.davidjeremiah.org/radio/archives?bid=4330.
7. Jessica Stewart, "Grieving Father Creates Touching Memorial for His Disabled Son," My Modern Met, May 19, 2017, https://mymodernmet.com/matthew-stanford-robison-memorial/.
8. Jeremiah, *The Book of Signs*, 212.

Chapter 8: Crowned by Christ

1. Armani Syed, "Here's the Full Schedule for King Charles III's Coronation—and What to Expect," *Time*, updated May 6, 2023, https://time.com/6274001/king-charles-iii-coronation-schedule/.
2. Francis Brown, S. R. Driver, and Charles A. Briggs, *A Hebrew and English Lexicon of the Old Testament* (Oxford, UK: Clarendon Press, 1952; repr., 1974), 139–139. Quoted in Gary Smalley and John Trent, *The Blessing: Giving the Gift of Unconditional Love and Acceptance* (Nashville, TN: Thomas Nelson, 1989), 26.
3. Used by permission.

Chapter 9: A Marriage Made in Heaven

1. Hayyim Schauss, "Ancient Jewish Marriage," The Jewish Telegraphic Agency, https://www.myjewishlearning.com/article/ancient-jewish-marriage/.
2. Zola Levitt, *A Christian Love Story* (Dallas, TX: Great Impressions Printing, 1978), 3.

Chapter 10: After the Saints Go Marching In

1. Charles Swindoll, *Steadfast Christianity: A Study Guide of 2 Thessalonians* (Fullerton, CA: Insight for Living, 1986), 24.
2. For a list of the names see Hitchcock, *The End*, 235–237.
3. Matt. 24–25, Mark 13, Luke 21.

Chapter 11: Now That the Chaos Has Come

1. David J. MacLeod, "The Lion Who Is a Lamb: An Exposition of Revelation 5:1–7," Bibliotheca Sacra (July-September 2007): 325–330, cited by Hitchcock, *The End*, 78; Amir Tsafarti, *Revealing Revelation* (Eugene, OR: Harvest Prophecy, 2022), 84; Charles Swindoll, *Swindoll's Living Insights New Testament Commentary: Revelation* (Wheaton, IL: Tyndale House, 2014), 102.
2. W. A. Criswell, *Expository Sermons on Revelation* (Grand Rapids, MI: Zondervan, 1960), 69–70.

Chapter 12: The Crowns and the Crimson

1. Alfred, Lord Tennyson, "In Memoriam A. H. H.," canto 131 (1850).
2. Blanchard, *Whatever Happened to Hell?*, 93.
3. "I Want a One Way Ticket to Heaven," audio CD, track 4 on Roy C, *Let's Go Back to God*, CD Baby, 2012.
4. Blanchard, *Whatever Happened to Hell?*, 93.
5. Figures vary widely. The figure 106 billion is cited at https://peopleandplanet.net/.
6. James Hamilton Jr., *Revelation: The Spirit Speaks to the Churches (Preaching the Word)* (Wheaton, IL: Crossway, 2012), 355.

Chapter 13: God Will Have His Garden

1. *State of the Bible: USA 2022*, American Bible Society, on Scripture engagement, https://scripture-engagement.org/content/state-of-the-bible-usa-2022/.

Chapter 14: Where the Soul Goes to Die

1. John MacArthur, *MacArthur New Testament Commentary: Revelation 12–22* (Chicago: Moody Press, 2000), 245.

2. Robert Jeffress, *Hell? Yes! And Other Outrageous Truths You Can Still Believe* (Colorado Springs, CO: Waterbrook Press, 2004), 71–72.
3. Blanchard, *Whatever Happened to Hell?*, 105.
4. James Denny, *Studies in Theology* (London: Hodder and Stoughton, 1904), quoted in Bruce Demarest, *The Cross and Salvation: The Doctrine of Salvation* (Wheaton, IL: Crossway Books, 1997), 31.
5. Luke 12:47–48; Matt. 10:15; Matt. 11:22, 24; Alfred N. Martin and Fred Zaspel, "Degrees of Punishment in Hell," The Gospel Coalition, https://www.thegospelcoalition.org/essay/degrees-punishment-hell/.
6. For a helpful resource on the duration of hell consult *Four Views on Hell*, Preston Sprinkle, general ed. (Grand Rapids, MI: Zondervan, 2016).
7. Blanchard, *Whatever Happened to Hell?*, 298.

Chapter 15: Finally, Home

1. *Vine's Complete Expository Dictionary of Old and New Testament Words* (Nashville: Thomas Nelson, 1985), 430–431.
2. Hitchcock, The End, 451
3. Wilbur M. Smith, "Revelation," *The Wycliffe Bible Commentary*, eds. Charles F. Pfeiffer and Everett F. Harrison (Chicago: Moody Press, 1962), 1522, quoted in Tom Constable, *Notes on Revelation*, 2017 ed., 234.
4. Alcorn, *Heaven*, 242.
5. John Phillips, *Exploring Revelation* (1974; rev. Grand Rapids, MI: Kregel Publications, 2001), 254.

Afterword: Made for More

1. *As Good as It Gets*, directed by James L. Brooks (Culver City, CA: TriStar Pictures, 1997).
2. *Vine's Expository Dictionary of Bible Words*, s.v. "seek" (Nashville, TN: Thomas Nelson, 1985), 558.
3. Spiros Zodhiates, ed., *The Hebrew-Greek Key Word Study Bible* , NASB 1977 ed., s.v. "set" (Chattanooga, TN: AMG Publishers, 2008), 5426.
4. A. Gordon Nasby, ed. *1041 Sermon Illustrations, Ideas and Expositions* (Grand Rapids, MI: Baker Book House, 1953), entry #282, 102.
5. C. S. Lewis, *The Voyage of the Dawn Treader* (New York: Scholastic, 1952), 180.
6. Jimmy Evans, *Tipping Point: The End Is Here* (Southlake, TX: XO Publishing, 2020), 190.

Inspired by what you just read?

Connect with Max

UPWORDS

The nonprofit teaching ministry of Max Lucado

Listen to Max's teaching ministry, UpWords, on the radio and online. Visit MaxLucado.com for more resources for spiritual growth and encouragement, including:

- Archives of UpWords, Max's daily radio program, and a list of radio stations where it airs
- Daily devotionals and emails from Max
- *The Max Lucado Encouraging Word Podcast*
- Video teaching and articles
- Online store with information on new books and special offers

1-800-822-9673
UpWords Ministries
P.O. Box 692170
San Antonio, TX 78269-2170
info@maxlucado.com

MaxLucado.com

Join the Max Lucado community:
Facebook.com/MaxLucado
Instagram.com/MaxLucado
X.com/MaxLucado
YouTube.com/MaxLucadoOfficial

HEAVEN'S TIME LINE

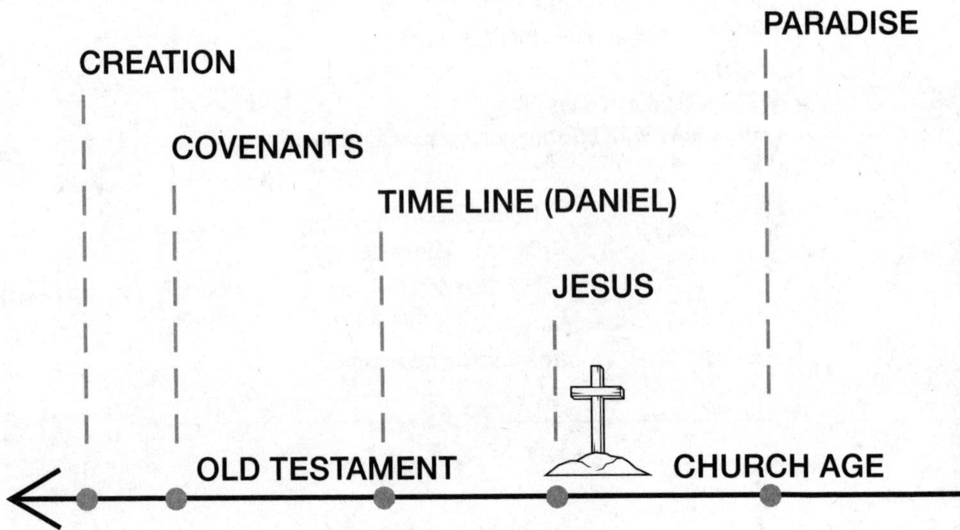

NOT TO SCALE

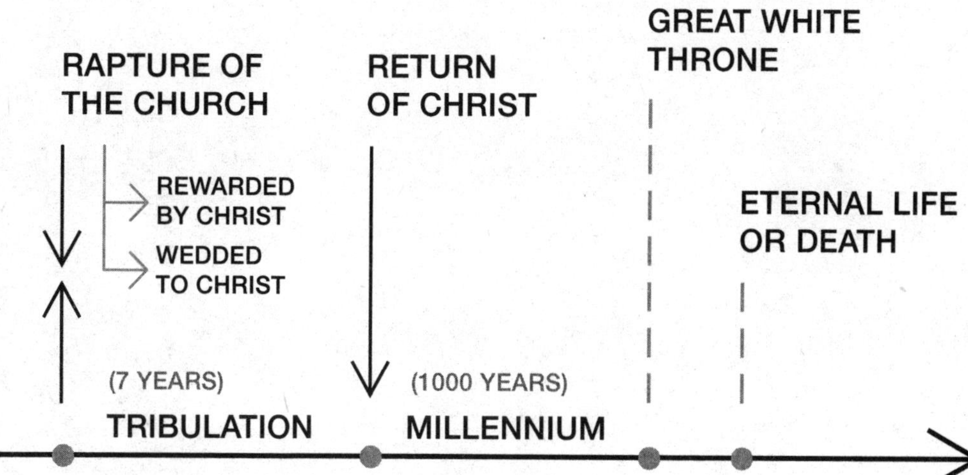
RAPTURE OF THE CHURCH
REWARDED BY CHRIST
WEDDED TO CHRIST
(7 YEARS)
TRIBULATION
RETURN OF CHRIST
(1000 YEARS)
MILLENNIUM
GREAT WHITE THRONE
ETERNAL LIFE OR DEATH